my revision notes

AQA A-level

POLITICS

US AND COMPARATIVE POLITICS

Rowena Hammal and Simon Lemieux

HODDER
EDUCATION
AN HACHETTE UK COMPANY

Although every effort has been made to ensure that website addresses are correct at time of going to press, Hodder Education cannot be held responsible for the content of any website mentioned in this book. It is sometimes possible to find a relocated web page by typing in the address of the home page for a website in the URL window of your browser.

Hachette UK's policy is to use papers that are natural, renewable and recyclable products and made from wood grown in well-managed forests and other controlled sources. The logging and manufacturing processes are expected to conform to the environmental regulations of the country of origin.

Orders: please contact Bookpoint Ltd, 130 Park Drive, Milton Park, Abingdon, Oxon OX14 4SE. Telephone: (44) 01235 827827. Fax: (44) 01235 400401. Email education@ bookpoint.co.uk Lines are open from 9 a.m. to 5 p.m., Monday to Saturday, with a 24-hour message answering service. You can also order through our website: www.hoddereducation.co.uk

ISBN: 978 1 5104 4766 0

© Rowena Hammal and Simon Lemieux 2019

First published in 2019 by

Hodder Education
An Hachette UK Company
Carmelite House
50 Victoria Embankment
London EC4Y 0DZ

www.hoddereducation.co.uk

Impression number 10 9 8 7 6 5 4 3 2

Year   2023   2022   2021   2020   2019

Typeset by Integra Software Services Pvt. Ltd., Pondicherry, India
Printed in Spain

A catalogue record for this title is available from the British Library.

Get the most from this book

Everyone has to decide his or her own revision strategy, but it is essential to review your work, learn it and test your understanding. These Revision Notes will help you to do that in a planned way, topic by topic. Use this book as the cornerstone of your revision and don't hesitate to write in it personalise your notes and check your progress by ticking off each section as you revise.

Tick to track your progress

Use the revision planner on pages 4–7 to plan your revision, topic by topic. Tick each box when you have:
- revised and understood a topic
- tested yourself
- practised the exam questions and gone online to check your answers and complete the quick quizzes

You can also keep track of your revision by ticking off each topic heading in the book. You may find it helpful to add your own notes as you work through each topic.

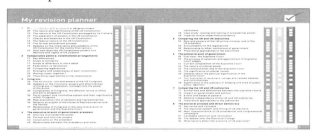

Features to help you succeed

Exam tips

Expert tips are given throughout the book to help you polish your exam technique in order to maximise your chances in the exam.

Typical mistakes

The author identifies the typical mistakes candidates make and explains how you can avoid them.

Now test yourself

These short, knowledge-based questions provide the first step in testing your learning. Answers are at the back of the book.

Definitions and key words

Clear, concise definitions of essential key terms are provided where they first appear.

Key words from the specification are highlighted in bold throughout the book.

Revision activities

These activities will help you to understand each topic in an interactive way.

Summaries

The summaries provide a quick-check bullet list for each topic.

Exam practice

Practice exam questions are provided for each topic. Use them to consolidate your revision and practise your exam skills.

Online

Go online to check your answers to the exam questions and try out the extra quick quizzes at **www.hoddereducation.co.uk/ myrevisionnotesdownloads**

My revision planner

REVISED   TESTED   EXAM READY

REVISED   TESTED   EXAM READY

REVISED TESTED EXAM READY

REVISED   TESTED   EXAM READY

Now test yourself answers

Exam practice answers and quick quizzes at
www.hoddereducation.co.uk/myrevisionnotesdownloads

Countdown to my exams

1 The constitutional framework of US government

The US Constitution is:
- the supreme authority in all aspects of US government: it has **constitutional sovereignty**
- codified and also hard to amend formally
- based around the separation of powers and checks and balances
- federal, with power shared between central/federal government and individual states, but federal law always has ultimate authority over any state laws (supremacy clause in the Constitution).

It established a republican form of government, i.e. a president, not a monarch, as head of state.

> **Constitutional sovereignty**
> Ultimate power (sovereignty) lies in the Constitution, not with the legislature as is the case in the UK.

The nature and significance of the US Constitution

Key principles

REVISED

The US Constitution was influenced by the ideas of the French philosopher Montesquieu (1689–1755). It was drawn up in 1787 in Philadelphia and ratified in 1788, replacing the much weaker **Articles of Confederation**.
- It was designed to avoid tyranny, especially by the leader, and so power is both separated and overlapping between the different branches of government: executive (presidency), legislature (Congress) and judiciary (Supreme Court).
- Each branch also **checks and balances** the other. For example, the president may veto an act of Congress, but Congress can impeach (remove) the president and override the veto.
- The main original document sets out the respective powers of each branch of government and also aspects of the political process, such as indirect election of the president and representation rules for Congress.
- Most aspects dealing with the protection of individual rights and freedoms are found in the amendments starting with the **Bill of Rights**.

The US Constitution was essentially a compromise between:
- those who wanted a stronger central government (**Federalists** such as Alexander Hamilton and John Adams) and those who wanted most power to rest with the states, e.g. Thomas Jefferson
- large states such as Virginia and small states such as Rhode Island – hence, small states had equal representation in the Senate (two senators per state irrespective of population size), while the number of seats in the House of Representatives is determined by population
- slave and non-slave states – slave states were allowed to count slaves as three-fifths of a free person for the purposes of calculating the size of a state delegation in the House of Representatives.

> **Articles of Confederation**
> The original constitution of the USA drawn up in 1777 and ratified in 1781. It had a weak central government and soon proved unsuited to the fledgling nation.
>
> **Checks and balances** The process by which different branches of government are limited or checked by the others, thus ensuring no one branch becomes too powerful. This principle is analysed in greater depth on p. 11.
>
> **Bill of Rights** The first ten amendments to the constitution passed in 1791. They are discussed more fully on p. 13.
>
> **Federalists** Those Founding Fathers who wanted a stronger central government. Arguably the first example of party and faction in the United States.

The nature of the US Constitution envisaged by its framers

The framers had a vision for the Constitution:

- The different branches would cooperate and make compromises with each other.
- No one branch of government would become too powerful. The desire was to avoid an over-powerful 'tyranny', as many Americans perceived the British monarchy to be in the late eighteenth century.
- A suspicion of democracy which was associated with mob rule. Nowhere in the original Constitution was the right even of 'one free (white) man, one vote' laid out. Nor were the president or Senate to be elected directly. Originally, senators were to be chosen by state governments; the Senate switched to direct elections only in 1913 (Seventeenth Amendment).
- It would be permanent and longlasting, hence it was made deliberately difficult to amend/formally change.

Typical mistake

The three-fifths clause was purely a means of calculating the number of representatives each state could send to the House. It did not give any slaves the vote, nor did it mean that an African-American slave was 'worth' three-fifths of a free person.

The separation of powers in the US Constitution

Power is separated by the US Constitution in the ways laid out in Table 1.1.

Exam tip

Although we often talk of the separation of powers in the USA, it is actually more accurate to refer to shared powers and separate personnel. For example, law making involves the cooperation of both president and Congress.

Table 1.1 **Separation of powers in the US Constitution**

President	<ul><li>Is commander-in-chief of the armed forces.</li><li>Oversees foreign policy and relations with foreign powers.</li><li>Is in charge of the federal bureaucracy and chooses secretaries of state (ministers).</li><li>Can issue pardons to individuals.</li><li>Nominates judges.</li><li>Can suggest laws to Congress and can also veto them.</li><li>Cannot sit in Congress, nor can members of their cabinet.</li></ul>
Congress	<ul><li>Passes laws and raises taxes.</li><li>Must confirm most presidential appointments (Senate only).</li><li>Ratifies foreign treaties and formal declarations of war.</li><li>Can **impeach** the president and judges.</li><li>Cannot serve in government, so must resign if appointed to the executive by the president. Hence Jeff Sessions had to resign as senator for Alabama when appointed by Trump as attorney general in 2017.</li></ul>
Supreme Court	<ul><li>Interprets the Constitution.</li><li>Ensures the actions of Congress and the president are in accordance with the Constitution.</li><li>Can 'strike down' laws/actions it sees as unconstitutional.</li></ul>

Exceptions to the principle of the separation of powers

REVISED

Exceptions include:

- the vice president is also president of the Senate and has the casting vote in the event of a tie
- the president's power of pardon is a judicial rather than executive power
- control and deployment of the armed forces: the president is commander-in-chief but Congress must authorise any declaration of war.

Impeachment The power of Congress to remove either the president or a member of the judiciary. It requires a simple majority in the House to formally begin the process; the actual trial is held in the Senate, with a two-thirds majority required for conviction.

1 Is the US Constitution unitary or federal?
2 When and where was the US Constitution drawn up?
3 How was the Constitution a compromise between slave and free states?
4 Which branch of government has the power of impeachment?
5 Which branch of government is in charge of foreign relations?

Answers on p. 125

Revision activity

Use Tables 1.2–1.4 and any other resources/ notes to create a diagram that shows more visually how each branch of government is checked and balanced by the other branches.

Checks and balances

Power in the US Constitution is checked and balanced in the ways outlined in Tables 1.2–1.4.

Table 1.2 **Checks and balances – powers of the president**

Powers of president	Limits	Example
Vetoes acts passed by Congress	Congress can overturn vetoes on a two-thirds vote in each chamber.	In 2016, Congress overrode Obama's veto of the Justice Against Sponsors of Terrorism Act.
Appoints heads of government departments and federal judges	Senate can reject a nomination by a simple majority.	In 1987, the Senate rejected President Reagan's nominee Robert Bork as a Supreme Court justice.
Has charge of the armed forces (commander-in-chief)	Congress can refuse funds (power of the purse) and has passed laws to limit presidential actions, e.g. 1973 War Powers Act.	In 2002, Congress voted through the Iraq Resolution to allow President George W. Bush to undertake military action in Iraq. Without it, he would have been on dubious legal/constitutional ground.

Table 1.3 **Checks and balances – powers of Congress**

Powers of Congress	Limits	Example
Passing laws	President can veto laws.	President Obama vetoed the Keystone XL Pipeline Approval Act in 2015.
Impeachment	Requires a high threshold of votes in the Senate to convict.	The Senate failed to impeach President Clinton in 1999.
Ratifying foreign treaties	Presidents bypass formal treaties, for example by making executive treaties.	The nuclear deal with Iran in 2015 was made without congressional approval by President Obama.

Table 1.4 **Checks and balances – powers of the Supreme Court**

Powers of Supreme Court	Limits	Example
Striking down laws passed by Congress as unconstitutional (**judicial review**)	Congress can pass a constitutional amendment (though this is far from easy).	In 1913, the Thirteenth Amendment permitted a federal income tax following an earlier Supreme Court case (*Pollock* v *Farmers' Loan & Trust Co.*).
	The Supreme Court cannot initiate cases of its own accord.	Same-sex marriage was legalised across America only when a case (*Obergefell* v *Hodges*) came before the Supreme Court.
	The president can alter the political composition of the Court via appointments when vacancies arise. With the support of Congress, they could enlarge (pack) the Court.	FDR tried to 'pack' the Supreme Court in the 1930s when it struck down some of his New Deal programmes. Congress refused to back him though.

6 What majority is needed in Congress to overturn a presidential veto?
7 How can a president bypass formal treaties that require congressional approval?
8 Why is judicial review such an important power of the Supreme Court?
9 Give an example of a presidential nominee for the Supreme Court being rejected by the Senate.
10 How can Congress check the power of the Supreme Court?

Answers on p. 125

> **Judicial review** The power of the Supreme Court to review laws and actions to judge whether they are compatible with the Constitution. Not specifically mentioned in the Constitution itself, the practice emerged from the 1803 *Marbury* v *Madison* case.

The federal nature of the US Constitution

Power in the USA is also restricted by a division of powers between federal (central) government and the states. This is known as **federalism**.

- The Tenth Amendment states that powers not held by the federal government shall reside with individual states.
- States retain a considerable number of powers, including:
  - power over local taxes such as sales tax and local property taxes
  - aspects of their election process, including whether to use primaries or caucuses to select candidates
  - whether or not to have the death penalty.
- Since the 1930s and President Franklin Roosevelt's New Deal, power has clearly shifted towards federal government and away from the individual states.
- There is often a clash between policies/laws made in Washington DC and individual states. For example, in the 1950s and 1960s, many conservative states in the Deep South strongly resisted efforts to desegregate. More recently, liberal states and cities such as San Francisco have opposed President Trump's demands to round up and deport illegal immigrants (the sanctuary cities movement).
- There is sometimes a direct clash between state and federal law. For example, federal law prohibits the cultivation and sale of marijuana. Yet the drug has been legalised in a number of states, including California. Although federal law in theory has the last word, on the ground it is very difficult to enforce.

> **Federalism** The notion that power is shared between central (federal) government and the 50 individual states.

> **Exam tip**
>
> When answering a question about federalism, aim to demonstrate an awareness of how power has shifted towards the federal government since the 1930s, under both Republican and Democrat presidents. This is despite efforts in the 1980s and 1990s to push back the role of 'big government', a movement often known as 'new federalism'.

The formal amendment process

There are only 27 formal amendments to the US Constitution. The last major one was in 1971, which lowered the voting age to 18.

- Formal amendments are difficult to pass. They require a two-thirds majority in both houses of Congress and then ratification by three-quarters of states, often within a set time limit.
- Over the centuries, thousands of amendments have been proposed, but most have failed. Among notable failures is the Equal Rights Amendment, which would have guaranteed gender equality. Passed by Congress, it then failed to secure ratification by enough states in time (1982), falling three states short of the required number.

The Bill of Rights 1791

The Bill of Rights comprises the first ten amendments to the US Constitution. It contains most of the key individual rights of American citizens found in the Constitution.

- Key rights include the First Amendment right to freedom of expression and the Sixth Amendment right to a fair and speedy trial.
- It has been the basis for much debate and interpretation since its adoption – for example, the death penalty and the Eighth Amendment that bans 'cruel and unusual punishment'.

The informal amendment process

As the US Constitution is so problematic to amend formally, in practice many changes are made informally, above all via rulings of the Supreme Court. In these cases, new rights are 'discovered' within the existing wording. Examples include:

- *Roe* v *Wade*, which granted American women some access to abortion using the 'due process clause' of the Fourteenth Amendment in 1973
- the *Citizens United* case in 2010, which extended to corporations and other groups First Amendment rights so that they could spend money more freely on election campaigns.

Debates on the importance and suitability of the US Constitution for the twenty-first century

Although it was the founding document of the USA, there has been much debate over the effectiveness of the US Constitution for modern times. Some of these issues are summarised in Table 1.5.

Table 1.5 **The US Constitution: criticisms and defences**

Criticisms of the US Constitution	Defences of the US Constitution
It is too difficult to amend and change easily.	It provides stability and continuity. It is also relatively easy to amend and update informally.
Some of its terms are vague and imprecise.	Lack of precision in its wording enables interpretations to adjust to changing times and cultures.
Some powers overlap and conflict, e.g. over foreign policy.	Such an overlap should encourage the different branches to work together. When clashes or gridlock occur (as with government shutdowns in 2018), blame partisan politicians, not the Constitution itself.
Not all rights are equally protected, e.g. race but not gender or disability.	Blame politicians and law makers again. The provision is there to make such amendments. Also, rights are protected in other ways, such as by Acts of Congress.
Specific clauses are outdated and/or unhelpful, e.g. biennial elections to the House and the right to gun ownership.	Again, blame politicians. Unhelpful/outdated sections of the Constitution can be removed, such as the one dealing with Prohibition when, in 1933, the Twenty-First Amendment repealed the Eighteenth Amendment.

→

Criticisms of the US Constitution	Defences of the US Constitution
Too much political power is given to the unelected Supreme Court: 'The US Constitution is what the Supreme Court says it is.'	These criticisms are normally made by the losing side in any major controversy. In reality, perhaps it is better to leave contentious and divisive issues such as gun rights, abortion and LGBT rights in the hands of legal experts rather than those of partisan politicians open to all kinds of influences.
It has become a focus for division and disunity in modern America.	The Constitution itself is still revered by nearly all Americans, even among those who disagree over what it means in places. Rewriting or substantially changing it would provoke more, not less, division in the States.
No other country has copied the US Constitution.	No other country is quite like the USA!

Now test yourself

TESTED

11 Look at the following statements about the US Constitution. Which are criticisms and which are statements in support of it?
(a) It has lasted for over 200 years and witnessed huge changes in American society and culture.
(b) The powers of the president are often too great in reality – for example, US presidents often undertake military action without congressional approval.
(c) The justices of the Supreme Court are not really that impartial – after all, they are political appointees.
(d) There are often clashes between the executive and the legislature – for example, the 16-day shutdown in 2013 and a 3-day one in January 2018, when there was no agreement over the federal budget.
(e) American citizens have the individual right to own guns.

Answers on p. 125

How well does the US Constitution protect civil liberties and rights of US citizens?

The US Constitution could be said to protect civil liberties and rights since:
- there are entrenched and **inalienable** rights found within, especially in the Bill of Rights
- these rights include: freedom of expression, the right to a fair trial, equal protection under the law and no bar to having the vote due to race or colour
- the Supreme Court in its decisions has often extended and expanded these rights, for example ending segregation (*Brown* v *Topeka* 1954) and allowing same-sex marriage (*Obergefell* v *Hodges* 2015)
- having rights and liberties enshrined in a single document makes them easy to access and understand. Most Americans have a clear idea of their individual rights and defend them fiercely.

> **Inalienable** Permanent, cannot be taken away.

The US Constitution could be said to be a poor defender of civil liberties and rights since:
- some rights are much better protected than others – gun owners have their right to bear arms entrenched in the Second Amendment, while no entrenched rights exist for women and children
- the Constitution is difficult to update and modernise – too much therefore relies upon informal amendment by the Supreme Court

> **Exam tip**
>
> When referring to rights and liberties protected in the US Constitution, either formally or informally, aim to include the specific amendment number or the relevant court case and year.

- the Supreme Court can and does change its opinions, for example over racial segregation and homosexuality. Thus, many rights are not permanent and entrenched, but are at the mercy of the Supreme Court, which is itself unelected and unaccountable to the people
- much of the Constitution is not concerned with protecting individual liberties so much as with setting out the workings of government. It is no substitute for a comprehensive and modern human rights charter that is fully inclusive and reflective of modern America.

Summary

You should now have an understanding of:
- the key principles enshrined in the US Constitution
- the importance and significance of the separation of powers
- the importance and significance of checks and balances
- the balance of power between the individual states and the federal government
- how the US Constitution can be amended both formally and informally
- the importance of the Bill of Rights
- the debate over how well the US Constitution works in contemporary America
- how well civil liberties and rights are protected by the US Constitution.

Exam practice

1 Explain and analyse three ways in which the US Constitution reflects the separation of powers. [9]
2 Explain and analyse three ways in which the Bill of Rights protects the rights of US citizens. [9]
3 Analyse, evaluate and compare the arguments in the passage below for and against the view that the US Constitution is outdated and needs replacing. [25]

> The US Constitution is essentially a product of its time. Drafted by exclusively white, male and Christian groups of property owners, it does little to defend the rights of ordinary citizens in the twenty-first century. There are no real protections of individual rights in the original document and the Bill of Rights likewise failed to protect certain key rights. It has proved fiendishly difficult to amend and many key groups such as women have little or no protection as a result. Compared with other constitutions and documents such as the United Nations' Universal Declaration of Human Rights, the US Constitution is a poor, outdated and occasionally harmful protector of citizens' rights. It also contains major flaws in terms of the political process, such as the need for agreement between the different branches of government. In today's age of hyper-partisanship, it has proved impossible to prevent gridlock. Thus, in October 2013, Americans were treated to the unedifying spectacle of many non-essential public services, such as national parks, being shut down because of the inability of a Democrat president and a Republican-controlled Congress to agree a budget. However, many would apportion blame here to politicians on both sides, not to the Founding Fathers. It is little wonder, then, that many Americans still have a touching reverence for the current constitution and do not want something more modern and formally flexible in its place. Again, in practice, the US Constitution has managed to evolve and adapt over time. While not entrenched, in reality the rights of many minority groups such as LGBT Americans are protected in the States. The case for replacement is far from clear cut.

Source: original material written by the author of this book for educational purposes, 2018

Answers and quick quiz online

ONLINE

2 Comparative politics: constitutional arrangements

Key differences

There are various differences between the US and UK constitutions:
- The US Constitution is codified, while that of the UK is not.
- The US Constitution is sovereign; in the UK, Parliament is sovereign: constitutional versus parliamentary sovereignty.
- Constitutional sovereignty gives the US Supreme Court considerable political power as it interprets the Constitution: judicial review.
- The UK Constitution is more flexible to amend, requiring only an act of Parliament. The formal amendment procedure in the USA is complex and requires a high threshold of political support.
- Federalism is embedded in the US Constitution, which is not the case in the UK with devolution.

> **Exam tip**
>
> Although this comparative topic is about comparing constitutions, it also requires knowledge from your study of the legislatures in both countries, plus material from the devolution topic studied for the UK paper.

Areas of similarity

There are also similarities:
- Both embrace the principles of representative government and democracy.
- Both in reality have evolved and developed over time.
- Each provides for an independent judiciary and some separation of powers/institutions.
- Each seeks to protect the individual rights of its citizens.
- In neither is power found exclusively in central or federal government.

The constitutions of the USA and the UK therefore display considerable contrasts but also share some features.

> **Exam tip**
>
> Ensure you are aware of similarities as well as differences in all your comparative topics. It is easy but unwise just to focus on the differences.

Areas of difference in more detail

Tables 2.1–2.4 outline the various differences between the two constitutions.

Sources and structure

REVISED

Table 2.1 Differences in structure

US Constitution	UK Constitution
Single codified document.	Has several sources, e.g. 1689 Bill of Rights, statute law such as the 1832 Representation of the People Act and common law. Uncodified.
Drawn up at one time (1787) and subsequently formally amended only infrequently.	Evolved over the centuries. Some sources, e.g. Magna Carta, go back to the Middle Ages. Frequently amended.
Formal amendment is difficult and complex.	Easy to alter via Acts of Parliament.
Republican, with an (indirectly) elected head of state. The president is highly active and politically partisan.	The UK remains a constitutional monarchy with an unelected head of state, whose role is ceremonial, not political.

Typical mistake

Do not say that the UK Constitution is unwritten. Rather, it is found in several places and is uncodified.

Nature and authority

REVISED

Table 2.2 **Differences in powers**

US Constitution	UK Constitution
Is sovereign, ultimate source of authority. Supreme Court has the ultimate power of interpretation: the Constitution is what the judges say it is.	Parliament is sovereign: the Constitution is what the Westminster Parliament chooses it to be.
Formal system of checks and balances, thus presidents can find it hard to push through legislation in Congress. Frequent gridlock.	Few formal checks and balances, thus prime ministers can often dominate the legislature. Can lead to accusations of an 'elective dictatorship'.
Embodies a separation of powers, or at least separate personnel and shared powers, e.g. members of the executive cannot be members of the legislature.	Very much reflects a fusion of powers. The executive is drawn entirely from the legislature. However, the judiciary in recent times has become institutionally separate with the creation of the UK Supreme Court.
Many citizens' rights are entrenched and inalienable and found mainly in the 1791 Bill of Rights (first ten amendments).	Citizens' rights are mainly protected by parliamentary legislation, e.g. the Human Rights Act (1998), and also by common law.
Makes clear provision for a sharing of powers between federal government and the states. Federalism is an inherent characteristic.	No express provision for federalism, favours a unitary style of government. Devolution has created a quasi-federal model, but in theory could be reversed by legislation.
Essentially a compromise in many ways, e.g. balancing the rights of small and large states in terms of congressional representation – the Connecticut Compromise.	Much more emphasis on unitary and centralised government.

Separation of powers

REVISED

Table 2.3 **Separation of powers**

US Constitution	UK Constitution
A fundamental principle, e.g. each branch is outlined in separate articles of the Constitution. A tendency towards regarding power with suspicion and thus a desire to spread it around institutions and individuals.	Not a fundamental principle and in part reflects a monarchical system of power being concentrated in the hands of the few, not the many. Existence of the royal prerogative conveys considerable power to the prime minister, such as the appointment and removal of ministers.
Formal separation of institutions, though in reality many powers are shared, e.g. legislation.	Less separation of institutions. The executive also sits in the legislature, though the judiciary is now completely separate.
Federalism also enhances a separation and dilution of powers. Power is shared, albeit unevenly, in many areas of policy between federal and state government.	Changes since 1997 have led to greater powers for the regions and a loss of power at Westminster (devolution), but it is debatable how far this constitutes an inalienable transfer of power.

Checks and balances

Table 2.4 Checks and balances

US Constitution	UK Constitution
Again, a fundamental principle; plenty of scope for one branch of government to check another, e.g. presidential veto.	Fewer formal checks and balances. Main threats and limits to a prime minister's powers come from opposition within their own party (e.g. Margaret Thatcher and the poll tax) or lack of an overall parliamentary majority (e.g. Theresa May's government elected in 2017).
Supreme Court can strike down executive actions or federal laws as unconstitutional, e.g. 1996 Defense of Marriage Act in the 2015 *Obergefell* v *Hodges* case.	No such provision, but the UK Supreme Court can declare laws and executive actions as 'incompatible' with the Human Rights Act or with EU law, e.g. Factortame case.
Provides for biennial elections to Congress (whole of the House and a third of the Senate). Makes Congress more accountable to voters and thus acts as a frequent check on both the executive and the legislature. Voters often use **mid-term elections** as a verdict on presidential performance.	The 2011 Fixed-Term Parliaments Act in theory means there should normally be a five-year gap between general elections. In reality, this can be easily bypassed, as in 2017.
Congress cannot directly override a Supreme Court ruling without passing a constitutional amendment. This is usually very difficult to achieve – no major amendments have been passed since 1971.	The government can overturn a ruling that it has acted illegally (*ultra vires*) by passing fresh legislation. This is usually straightforward.

Revision activity

Reading through the material and your own notes, create an essay plan or spider gram that tackles the issue of which constitution best defends individual rights.

Mid-term elections Biennial elections for Congress that take place midway (i.e. two years) through a presidential term. They often result in losses for the president's party (protest vote) and losing control or influence in Congress, thereby making it harder for the president to push through controversial legislation.

Now test yourself

TESTED

1 Name an act of Congress ruled unconstitutional by the Supreme Court.
2 How do the two constitutions differ over the power of the judiciary?
3 Which constitution is easier to amend formally?
4 Which constitution makes it easier to check and make accountable the legislature?
5 Do both constitutions provide for elected bicameral legislatures?

Answers on p. 125

Federalism vs devolution

In essence, while both constitutions now seek to limit the power of central government, the US model is arguably much more successful and certainly better established. Federalism is also embedded in the US Constitution in a way that devolution is not.

Similarities

- Neither constitution originally embraced universal suffrage, so democracy has evolved over time – in the USA via amendments (e.g. the Nineteenth Amendment, enfranchising women), in the UK via statute law (e.g. in 1969 the voting age was lowered to 18).
- Both systems allow for many powers to be exercised and public services to be delivered at state/regional level. These include some local taxation, transport and education.
- Both enable local political traditions and trends to be reflected. Hence southern US states have stricter laws on abortion and laxer ones on the public display of firearms. Scotland has a more left-wing bias in some policy areas, e.g. higher taxes for the wealthiest and a greater investment in public services, such as free university tuition.
- Arguably the two systems are moving closer together: the UK has increased the powers of its devolved assemblies (quasi-federal system), while in the USA, federal government has encroached on some areas, such as education, traditionally reserved for states.

Key differences

- Federalism embraces all of the USA; devolution exists in only a minority of the UK and not in England itself.
- The US Constitution from the beginning envisaged a clear division and separation of powers between federal and states' government, e.g. the Tenth Amendment.
- Devolution in the UK is much more recent (1997) and entirely created by legislation. Devolution is essentially power delegated, not permanently and inalienably transferred. In practice, though, any attempt to reverse devolution in the regions would be highly problematic.
- The power of states in the USA is considerably greater, including controversial areas such as the death penalty.

Comparing legislatures

Similarities

- Both legislatures are the supreme law-making body and possess **legislative supremacy**. Thus, laws passed by states or devolved assemblies cannot conflict with those passed by Congress or Parliament.
- Both also check and scrutinise the executive via committees, investigations and debates.
- Each is bicameral.
- They are dominated by political parties.
- They contain members directly representing geographical areas.

> **Legislative supremacy** The laws made in Parliament/Congress possess the ultimate authority. No other legislatures such as state governments or devolved assemblies can pass laws that directly contradict or conflict with the national legislature.

Differences

Table 2.5 outlines the differences between the US Congress and the UK Parliament.

Table 2.5 **Differences between the legislatures**

US Congress	UK Parliament
Federal law can be struck down by the courts as unconstitutional.	**Parliamentary statutes** cannot be struck down by the courts, though they can be deemed 'incompatible' with the Human Rights Act. They must also (until 2019 at the earliest) be compatible with EU law.
Both chambers are directly elected.	Only the Commons is elected; the Lords is made up solely of appointed members (life peers, 92 hereditary peers and 26 bishops).
The chambers have equal legislative power.	The 1949 Parliament Act ensures the Lords must ultimately abide by the will of the Commons.
There can be congressional gridlock if both chambers fail to agree on a bill. This can often happen as different parties may control each chamber.	There is no possibility of gridlock: the Lords can only suggest amendments, which can be and often are overturned in the Commons. Weak governments can be defeated in Commons votes, however.
The legislature is separate to and independent of the executive. Scrutiny largely takes place in committees. Members of the executive can be forced to give evidence in congressional committee hearings.	The executive is found in the legislature, thus ministers are frequently and directly accountable to Parliament: the concept of ministerial accountability and also PMQs/ministerial questions.
The legislature can remove only individual members of the executive by impeachment and not the whole body.	The whole executive can be removed by a no-confidence motion in the Commons, leading to an early general election, as happened in 1979.

Strengths and weaknesses of each constitution

The US Constitution:

- is difficult to amend and is inflexible, but it can be and is amended informally via judicial review and interpretative amendments. Yet this arguably gives too much power to an unelected Supreme Court
- contains some wording that is vague and general, but this enables an essentially eighteenth-century document to evolve over time. Yet this can lead to conflict and division, e.g. over the precise meaning of the Second Amendment
- enables power to be shared and spread, but this can mean gridlock is common and it is difficult to pass reforms. Yet this is preferable to too much power being concentrated in one place.

The UK Constitution:

- is easy to change, but this can lead to a constantly changing political landscape. Overall change, though, has been evolutionary rather than revolutionary, as with the development of devolution
- does not have citizens' rights entrenched – they are protected mostly by statute law, which could be repealed, but this is unlikely and in any case the UK has signed up to the ECHR. Yet this too could be undone by government post Brexit
- gives the prime minister considerable power over Parliament and can usually dominate the legislative agenda, but this has led to accusations of 'presidential premiership'. Yet the most recent prime ministers, Cameron and May, have not wielded such power due to small/non-existent majorities.

Parliamentary statute A law passed by Parliament, known as an Act of Parliament.

Revision activity

After looking through the arguments that suggest the two constitutions are becoming more similar, write down, without looking at your notes or this book, what you think are still the key differences between them.

Moving closer together?

It could be argued that overall the constitutions of the UK and the USA are becoming more similar in some areas – see Table 2.6.

Table 2.6 Areas of similarity between the two constitutions

Codification	The UK Constitution is becoming increasingly codified, e.g. the Ministerial Code.
Federalism	Devolution has made the UK quasi-federal, while in the USA, federal government exerts increasing influence over states in areas such as education.
Role of the judiciary	The judiciary has had a more political role and higher profile in the UK, not least since the creation of the UK Supreme Court and the passage of the Human Rights Act in 1998.
Balance of power between the legislature and the executive	Recent premierships, those of Cameron and May, have been less 'imperial' than those of Blair and Thatcher, not least due to small/non-existent majorities in Parliament.
Entrenched rights	Arguably individual rights in the UK have become more embedded with the passage of measures such as the Human Rights Act.

Theoretical approaches to the constitutions

As part of your study of comparative politics, you need to be familiar with the three theoretical approaches to comparative politics:

- Structural – focuses on institutions and structures of the state. The key question posed by such an approach is what role or function a structure or institution (such as a political party, a constitution or a legislature) has within a country's political system. It also assumes that any change within the system affects other parts of the state as well.
- Rational – emphasises the role of the individual within a nation and assumes that they will normally act or make political choices in a logical way to maximise positive outcomes for themselves or their cause. There is a heavy emphasis on self-interest as a prime mover in political action.
- Cultural – places a lot of weight on the historical and sociological context when studying and comparing political systems. For example, the historic emphasis on limited government in the USA, or the greater acceptance of the hereditary and non-elected aspects of UK politics, such as the monarchy and the Lords.

Table 2.7 analyses the structural, rational and cultural aspects of the two constitutions.

Table 2.7 Roles of the two constitutions

	Aspects to analyse
Structural The role of political institutions	<ul><li>A codified US Constitution makes it more difficult to formally amend than in the UK.</li><li>Parliamentary sovereignty in the UK results in both a less powerful Supreme Court and legislature, as the courts cannot override a prime minister in the same way as in the USA and the prime minister usually dominates the legislature.</li><li>The direct election in the USA of both congressional chambers (since 1913) and their equal legislative powers can lead to disagreements and gridlock in a way not seen in the UK.</li><li>The US Constitution specifically provides for separate branches of government with enumerated powers that can overlap and conflict, e.g. in foreign policy and military action.</li></ul>

→

Rational The role of individuals	• The constitutional limits on the formal power of the president mean the president often has to use informal methods to exert authority, such as the 'power to persuade' and using the media to convey their message – 'bully pulpit'. Trump and Twitter! • Individual US Supreme Court judges are far more politicised than their UK counterparts and are traditionally, if slightly misleadingly, labelled as conservative (Clarence Thomas) or liberal (Ruth Bader Ginsburg). Such labels are not usually applied to UK judges. • The federalist nature of the US Constitution means that pressure groups are far more likely to lobby a range of institutions, e.g. state governments and bureaucracies. Most lobbying in the UK still focuses on Westminster, though devolved assemblies, local councils and EU institutions are increasingly targeted for certain issues. • The US Constitution gives the president a direct mandate (via the Electoral College) from the voters. In the UK, the PM relies much more on the loyalty of their MPs and the wider party. Their democratic mandate is indirect and reliant on parliamentary support. • Mid-term elections tend to encourage presidents to pass key legislation in the first two years, e.g. Obama and healthcare reform, Trump and tax cuts.
Cultural The role of shared ideas and culture	• The codification and entrenched rights of the US Constitution and the Bill of Rights reflect a clear desire by the Founding Fathers to limit the concentration of power and to preserve individual liberties. • The evolution and antiquity of the UK Constitution means it still contains aspects of a more feudal past, such as the House of Lords and the Royal Assent. • The entrenched rights in the US Constitution make most Americans keenly aware of their rights even though they might strongly disagree on how they are interpreted in practice. In the UK, there is a greater sense of leaving it to Parliament, though recourse to the courts to uphold rights perceived to be protected by the ECHR is increasingly common.

Now test yourself

TESTED

6 Read the statements below and decide which of the three theoretical approaches is most applicable.
   (a) The US Constitution deliberately embodies the separation of powers and checks and balances.
   (b) The UK prime minister rarely has to seek support for policies from opposition parties.
   (c) The courts in the USA are more powerful than those in the UK.
   (d) The hereditary principle still plays a part in the UK Constitution with the Lords and monarchy.
   (e) Pressure groups in the USA tend to lobby a wider range of institutions than in the UK.

Answers on p. 125

Summary

You should now have an understanding of:
• the key differences and similarities between the UK and US constitutions in terms of nature and structure, and how they are becoming more alike in some ways
• how power is checked and balanced in both constitutions
• how federalism differs from devolution
• key similarities and differences between the UK and US legislatures
• the overall advantages and disadvantages of each constitution
• how to apply the three theoretical approaches when comparing the UK and US constitutions.

Exam practice

1 Explain and analyse three ways in which structural theory could be used to study legislatures in the UK and the USA. [9]
2 'The US Constitution is more rigid and inflexible than that of the UK.' Analyse and evaluate this statement. [25]
3 'There is little difference in reality between federalism in the USA and devolution in the UK.' Analyse and evaluate this statement. [25]

Answers and quick quiz online

ONLINE

3 Congress

Congress is the legislative branch of the US government, responsible for legislation and oversight of the executive.

- In 2018, fewer than 20% of Americans approved of Congress's work.
- It will be seen that while Congress has significant powers, its effectiveness varies.

> **Congress** The federal legislature of the United States. It consists of two chambers: the House of Representatives and the Senate.

The structure, role and powers of the US Congress

Structure of Congress

REVISED

Congress is structured in the following way:

- It is bicameral (made up of two chambers).
- Congressional elections are held every two years.
- Senators serve six-year terms, representatives serve two-year terms.
- One third of **Senate** seats and all **House of Representatives** seats are contested at each election.

Congress was designed by the Founding Fathers as a compromise:

- Seats in the House of Representatives were allocated according to the population size of each state.
- This was intended to please larger states, by giving them more influence.
- Today, the most populous state in the USA is California, with 53 representatives in the House, while seven states have just one representative (e.g. Alaska).
- However, in the Senate, every state receives two seats, regardless of its size.
- This was intended to reassure smaller states that they would not be dominated by larger states.

> **Senate** The upper house of Congress. It has 100 members, called senators, who serve six-year terms. Each state has two senators.
>
> **House of Representatives** The lower house of Congress. It has 435 members, called representatives or congress(wo)men, who are elected for two-year terms. Members represent congressional districts within a state (unless the state has only one representative).

Roles of Congress

REVISED

Congress has the following roles:

- passing legislation
- representing the people
- overseeing the executive
- declaring war.

Powers of Congress

REVISED

The powers outlined in Table 3.1 help Congress to fulfil its different roles.

Table 3.1 The powers of Congress

Legislative powers (both houses)	• Congress initiates legislation. • Both houses must approve a bill. • Once a bill has been approved it is sent to the president's office where it will be signed, vetoed or left on his desk (it then automatically becomes law after ten days).
Overriding a presidential **veto**	• Congress can override the president's veto if it has a two-thirds majority in each house.
Initiating amendments to the constitution	• Any amendment to the constitution needs a two-thirds majority in both houses. • Once it passes Congress, the amendment is then sent to the states.
Ratifying treaties (Senate only)	• Presidents negotiate treaties, but they cannot be ratified (made official) without a two-thirds majority in the Senate.
Declaring war	• Approval is needed from both houses. • This power has not been used since 1941 (declaration of war on Japan). • Modern presidents avoid asking for a formal declaration of war.
Congressional oversight	• Congress approves federal budgets. • Congressional committees also allow congressional oversight and investigation of the executive.
Confirming presidential appointments (Senate only)	• Senate approval is required for many presidential appointments. • All presidential appointments to federal judiciary. • Most presidential appointments to federal government.
Impeachment and removal from office	• Only the House of Representatives can impeach a public official. • A simple majority in the House is needed for impeachment. • Only the Senate can try impeachments (conduct a formal trial). • A two-thirds majority in the Senate is needed for a guilty verdict. • This results in the official's immediate removal from office. • President Clinton was impeached in 1998 but found not guilty by the Senate in 1999.
Electing the president and vice president in the event of a hung Electoral College	• This occurs only if no candidate has an absolute majority in the Electoral College. • It has not been used since 1824.

Veto The refusal of the president to sign a bill passed by Congress. This means the bill will not become law.

Impeachment The charging of a public official with a crime. Impeachment is done by the House of Representatives. The Senate is responsible for carrying out the trial and finding the official guilty/not guilty.

Now test yourself

TESTED

1 How many members are there in the Senate and in the House?
2 What is the term for a legislature made up of two chambers?
3 What is a presidential veto?
4 What is impeachment?

Answers on p. 125

Debates on the functions, powers and effectiveness of Congress

Table 3.2 outlines the functions, powers and effectiveness of Congress.

Table 3.2 Functions, powers and effectiveness of Congress

	Functions	Powers	Effectiveness
Legislation	To initiate, debate, amend and pass legislation	● Either chamber can block legislation – the approval of both is needed for a bill to become law. ● Senators can filibuster a bill. ● The Senate needs 60 votes (a three-fifths super-majority) to invoke cloture. ● The president decides whether to sign, veto or leave the bill. ● In the event of a presidential veto, Congress decides whether to amend or abandon the bill, or to override the veto. ● A two-thirds majority in both chambers is required to override a presidential veto.	● Only 2–3% of all bills become law – this figure has fallen since the 1980s, when 6–7% of bills became law. ● Gridlock typically occurs if the House and the Senate are controlled by different parties as both chambers are equally powerful. ● Frequent use of filibusters allows members of the Senate to 'kill off' legislation. ● Increased use of 'closed rules' (rules that forbid amendments) means that Congress makes fewer amendments to bills, resulting in less improvement to legislation. ● Presidential vetoes are rarely overturned as a super-majority is needed.
Oversight	To oversee and investigate the activities of the government Not specifically mentioned in the Constitution: seen as an implied power	● Congressional committees hold hearings and investigate government actions. ● Congress can compel (subpoena) witnesses to provide information. ● Lying to Congress is a crime, with a possible prison sentence. ● Congress has an agency to investigate and audit the government: the Government Accountability Office (GAO). ● Congress can impeach and try government officials. ● Senate confirmation is needed for many executive nominees. ● Senate approval is needed to ratify treaties negotiated by the president.	● Oversight is typically weaker during periods when one party holds the presidency and both houses of Congress, as the majority members of Congress tend to be reluctant to criticise their president. ● It is stronger during periods of divided government, as the majority members of one or both houses of Congress have an incentive to investigate their opponents in the executive. ● Investigations can be intended to smear the political opposition with bad publicity, rather than being a positive form of oversight. ● Investigations can be lengthy and time-consuming, with few concrete results. ● It is difficult for an unpopular Congress to attack a popular president. ● Fear of congressional oversight helps to keep government acting effectively. ● Fear of impeachment helps to keep officials acting within the law. ● The confirmation process for political nominees is highly politicised and can lead to the Senate deliberately blocking a reasonable nomination. ● The Senate's power of ratification forces the president to work closely with the Senate during treaty negotiations.

	Functions	Powers	Effectiveness
Power of the purse	To ensure that the people's representatives give their consent to taxation	• Only Congress can raise revenue (tax people). • All tax bills must start in the House. • The Senate can amend tax bills. • The approval of both chambers is needed for the bill to become law.	• Congress can extract key concessions from the president in return for passing the budget. • If a compromise cannot be reached with the executive, Congress can refuse to pass the budget, resulting in government shutdown.

Revision activity

Read Table 3.2 and make a list of Congress's strengths and weaknesses.

Now test yourself

TESTED

5 What is a filibuster?
6 How can a filibuster be ended?
7 What is oversight?
8 What is the 'power of the purse'?

Answers on p. 125

Exam tip

When assessing the effectiveness of Congress, remember to consider how it is affected by the political context of the day. Congress will usually be less effective in passing legislation if the two chambers are held by opposing parties, whereas if the party of government also holds both houses of Congress, it is likely to perform less effective oversight.

Composition of Congress, the different terms of office and party allegiance

Composition of Congress

REVISED

Members of Congress have to meet the following criteria:
• Age – over 25 for congress(wo)men, over 30 for senators.
• Citizenship – congress(wo)men need to have been a US citizen for a minimum of seven years, senators for a minimum of nine years.
• Residency – must reside in the state they represent.

The composition of Congress has been criticised for failing to accurately represent US society. Table 3.3 shows the representation of different groups in the 115th Congress.

Table 3.3 **Representation in the 115th Congress (February 2018 figures)**

% of US population	House of Representatives	Senate
Women (51%)	19%	22%
African-Americans (13%)	11%	3%
Hispanic-Americans (18%)	9%	5%
Protestant faith (47%)	55%	58%
Catholic faith (21%)	33%	24%
Jewish faith (2%)	5%	8%
Muslim faith (0.9%)	0.5%	0%

- Many members of Congress first serve in the state legislatures, where women and African-Americans are also under-represented. This makes it difficult to increase numbers in Congress as there can be a shortage of suitable candidates.
- In 2018 more women ran for Congress than ever before, partly as a reaction against the defeat of Hillary Clinton and the election of Donald Trump.
- African-Americans and Hispanics are better represented in the House of Representatives than in the Senate. This is because the creation of **majority-minority districts** makes it easier for minority candidates to win seats in congressional districts where a majority of voters are from the same minority racial group.

Congress has also been criticised for the advanced age and narrow background of its members:
- In February 2018 the average age of members of the House of Representatives was 58 years.
- The average age of senators was 62 years.
- The main professions of members before entering Congress are law, politics and business.
- Members of Congress are also much better educated than the general population: in February 2018 all senators had a degree, as did 94% of congress(wo)men.

> **Majority-minority districts** Congressional district boundaries are drawn so that a majority of voters in the district are from the same minority group (e.g. African-Americans).

Terms of office

REVISED

Members of the Senate and members of the House of Representatives have different **terms of office**:
- Six years for senators.
- Two years for representatives.

There are several benefits of having terms of office of different lengths:
- Senators are in post longer, so they should become more experienced.
- Senators should be able to take a more long-term view of issues than congress(wo)men, as they do not need to face the public in elections as frequently.
- The composition of the House of Representatives can alter dramatically every two years, reflecting changes in public opinion.
- The House gives a more accurate representation of the politics of the nation at any given time, whereas the Senate acts as some protection against volatile swings in public opinion.

> **Term of office** Refers to how long a member of Congress can stay in their position before they must contest it in another election.

Party allegiance

REVISED

In Congress:
- all members of the House of Representatives are either Republican or Democrat
- all but two senators are either Republican or Democrat
- those two senators are independents, but they work closely with the Democrats (one of them, Senator Bernie Sanders of Vermont, even ran against Hillary Clinton in the 2016 presidential Democratic primaries).

Now test yourself

9　How do the terms of office for the Senate and the House differ?
10　What percentage of Congress is female?
11　Why are majority-minority districts important?
12　How many members of Congress are not a member of the two main parties?

Answers on p. 125

Party system and committee system and their significance within Congress

Party system

Congressional caucuses

Members of Congress belong to a congressional caucus.

- Republicans belong to either the House or Senate Republican caucus, Democrats to either the House or Senate Democratic caucus.
- Smaller congressional caucuses act as 'sub-groupings' of members with a similar interest to advance.
- This interest is often ideological, e.g. the House Freedom Caucus represents conservative Republicans with a commitment to limited government.
- Some congressional caucuses include members of both parties, e.g. the Bipartisan Heroin Task Force.
- Congressional caucuses may include members from both houses, e.g. the Congressional Black Caucus.
- Smaller caucuses can act as an alternative influence to the party leadership, e.g. the House Freedom Caucus opposed President Trump's budget at the start of 2018 – the Republicans had to depend on Democrats to pass the bill.

Party leadership

- Members of each party caucus elect a leader, known as the majority leader if their party has a majority in that chamber or the minority leader if they do not.
- The majority and minority leaders act as 'floor leaders' in both chambers, co-ordinating their parties for votes and debates, and the majority leaders plan the legislative agenda.
- The Speaker of the House of Representatives is the most high-profile leadership position in Congress.
- The Speaker is elected by all members of the House and is a member of the majority party.
- The Speaker presides over debates and keeps order in the House, determines the legislative agenda for the House, and chooses members of conference and select committees.
- The House majority leader follows the Speaker's agenda.
- If the Speaker is from a different party to that of the executive, he or she provides the main focus for opposition to the president.
- The Speaker is second only to the vice president in the line of presidential succession.

Party discipline

- Party discipline has traditionally been very weak.
- The separation of powers prevents party leaders from offering government positions to members of Congress in exchange for their support.
- The Speaker decides who sits on the House Rules Committee and who chairs select and conference committees.
- However, this provides only a limited incentive for members to conform to the party's wishes.
- As Congress has become more **partisan**, members have become more likely to vote along party lines.
- However, party leaders still lack the tools to discipline their membership if required.
- Despite controlling both houses, President Trump and House Speaker Paul Ryan struggled to persuade members of their own party to vote for the president's budget, resulting in two government shutdowns at the start of 2018.

> **Partisanship** A situation in which the political parties are strongly opposed to each other and have little common ground. It usually results in parties refusing to compromise or work together.

Typical mistake

Students may assume that party discipline in Congress is similar to that in the House of Commons, but there is a huge difference. The separation of powers means that presidents are not members of Congress, whereas the UK prime minister is an MP and leader of the biggest party in the House of Commons. The prime minister has much greater powers of patronage (see p. 47) and uses the whip system to maintain party discipline.

Partisanship

- Members of Congress have become increasingly polarised over the past two decades.
- In the 1980s many members were centrists, with considerable overlap between centrist Republicans and Democrats.
- The parties have moved away from each other – few representatives now remain in the centre of the political spectrum.
- This makes **bipartisanship** much more difficult and gridlock more likely during periods of divided government.
- **Party unity votes** have increased significantly since the turn of the century.

> **Bipartisanship** A situation in which Republicans and Democrats work together to achieve a common goal, e.g. passing legislation.
>
> **Party unity vote** A vote in which the majority of voting Republicans oppose the majority of voting Democrats.

Typical mistake

Do not confuse partisanship and party discipline. Partisanship simply means that the parties strongly oppose each other, whereas party discipline means that the party leadership is able to convince its members to vote in the way that it wishes. In February 2018 there was heated partisanship within Congress, but party discipline was poor. The House Freedom Caucus refused to vote for the government's budget, while some Democrats supported it despite minority leader Nancy Pelosi's opposition.

Exam tip

One of the most important political developments over the past two decades has been the rise in partisan politics in the USA. This is well worth emphasising in exam answers, as it explains why gridlock occurs frequently and presidents' increasing frustration with Congress. It also links to Congress's low approval ratings, as the decline of bipartisanship has made it harder to pass legislation, to the disappointment of voters.

Committee system

Table 3.4 outlines the **committee system** used by Congress.

> **Committee system** A system of different types of committee used by Congress to divide up its workload. Includes standing committees, select committees, the House Rules Committee and conference committees.

Table 3.4 **The committee system**

	Features	Functions	Significance
Standing committees	• Permanent. • Each focused on specific area of policy, e.g. foreign affairs. • Much of the work is done within sub-committees. • Parties are represented in the same proportions as in the Senate or House, so the majority party in a chamber has a majority on all standing committees for that chamber.	• Committee stage of bills: standing committees hold hearings, listen to and question witnesses, and vote on whether the bill should proceed to the House or the Senate. • Investigations and oversight: focused on the committee's policy area. • Considering presidential appointments (Senate only): hearings are followed by a committee vote on the nominee. This is a recommendation to the rest of the Senate on whether to confirm the appointment.	• Hearings are often high profile and attract media interest. • Long-term members of standing committees become experts in their policy area. • Committee chairs are influential. • Standing committees allow Congress to manage efficiently the wide range of issues that it needs to legislate on and investigate. • System provides crucial oversight of the executive.
Select committees	• Most are temporary. • Generally made up of members from one house.	• Usually to investigate a specific question, e.g. the House Select Committee on Benghazi (2014–16). • Prevents the relevant standing committee from being overloaded by a single urgent issue.	• Provides focused scrutiny and investigation of important issues. • Holds high-profile and detailed hearings in the public interest.
House Rules Committee	• A standing committee in the House of Representatives. • Small membership (13 members at the start of 2018). • Favours the majority party in a 2:1 ratio (at the start of 2018, 9 of the 13 members were Republicans).	• Sets the 'rules' for bills, determining how much time they will be given on the floor of the House and whether amendments will be allowed.	• This is the means by which the Speaker controls what is debated on the floor of the House. • The chair of the House Rules Committee is one of the key positions in Congress. • The committee has enormous power: it can determine what is discussed when, for how long and in what way.

	Features	Functions	Significance
			• The House can force a bill to be debated if an absolute majority of members sign a 'discharge petition', but this is not easy to achieve.
Conference committees	• Temporary – exist only to consider a specific bill. • Members come from both houses to sit on one committee.	• Consider two different versions of the same bill (one already passed by the Senate, one already passed by the House) and merge them into one combined bill. • The final version of the bill is sent back to both houses for approval.	• Important role in developing legislation. • Either or both houses can vote against the final bill. • Party leaders increasingly prevent bills from going to conference committee (where the shape of the final bill is out of their control) by asking members in one chamber to adopt the other chamber's bill.

Typical mistake

It is easy to confuse US and UK select committees. In the USA, select committees are usually temporary and set up to address a specific issue, e.g. the House Select Committee on Benghazi (2014–16). In the UK, select committees are permanent and generally focused on a particular area of policy, e.g. the Health Select Committee.

Now test yourself

TESTED ☐

13 What are majority and minority leaders?
14 What is the role of the Speaker of the House?
15 What are standing committees?
16 Why is the House Rules Committee important?

Answers on pp. 125–26

Representative role of senators and representatives

Individual members of Congress perform their representative function in the following ways:
• Communicating with their constituents through 'town hall' meetings, visits and social media, to ensure that they understand their constituents' views and can represent them in Congress.
• Debating, amending and voting on legislation. Representatives may vote according to their constituents' views (**delegate model**) or for what they believe are their constituents' best interests (**trustee model**).
• Sitting on relevant standing committees (e.g. Pat Roberts, the chair of the Senate Agricultural Committee, is the senator for Kansas, an agricultural state).
• Lobbying the government for funds or policies that would benefit their constituents (this is known as 'pork barrel politics' in the case of funding that is really unnecessary).

Delegate model
Representatives vote according to their constituents' wishes, ignoring their own judgement if it conflicts with that of their constituents.

Trustee model
Representatives should vote according to their best judgement, not their constituents' wishes. This assumes that representatives are better placed to make decisions than constituents as they have a better understanding of the issues.

● Using their congressional offices and staff to help constituents with problems, especially those involving a federal agency (this is known as constituency casework).

The whole of Congress also has a demographic representative function:
● This relates to how closely the whole of Congress reflects the gender, race, age and social background of America.
● Congress under-represents many key groups of voters, e.g. women and ethnic minorities (see pp. 26–27).

(see pp. 26–27)

Exam tip

Do not confuse the under-representation of many groups in Congress with the representative function of individual members of Congress. Individual members can represent their constituents effectively by listening to their views and reflecting these in their voting, even if Congress as a whole is not demographically representative of US society.

Relative strengths of the House of Representatives and the Senate

The House and the Senate have joint powers in the following key areas:
● legislation
● oversight
● overriding a presidential veto
● initiating amendments to the Constitution
● declaring war.

However, there are a few key areas in which they differ.

The House of Representatives and the Senate: a comparison

REVISED

Table 3.5 compares the powers of the House of Representatives and the Senate.

Table 3.5 The House of Representatives and the Senate: a comparison

Feature	House of Representatives	Senate
Confirming appointments	N/A	● Sole power to confirm appointments.
Ratifying treaties	N/A	● Sole power to ratify treaties negotiated by the president.
The power of the purse	● Only the House can initiate money bills.	● The Senate can amend money bills; in order to pass financial legislation, both chambers need to agree.
Impeachment	● The House has sole power of impeachment: it decides whether to charge an official with an offence.	● The Senate has sole power to try all impeachments: it decides whether an official is guilty.
Term of office	● Two years, so members are under greater pressure to keep their constituents happy.	● Six years, so members can focus more on their work as senators and less on running for re-election.
Career prospects	● There are 335 more congress-(wo)men than senators, so they face more competition for leadership posts and committee membership. ● Congress(wo)men may aim to be elected to the Senate. However, senators do not covet a position in the House, as it is seen as less desirable.	● Higher public profile as there are only two senators per state. ● Good opportunities to progress to leadership roles within the Senate and committees. ● Can be a route to the presidency: five presidents were former senators, e.g. Barack Obama. Many presidential candidates have also been senators, e.g. Hillary Clinton.

Revision activity

Look at Table 3.5 and rank the differences between the Senate and the House in order of significance. Decide how far it is true that the two chambers are equally powerful.

Relationship of Congress to the executive branch of government and the Supreme Court

Relationship to the executive
REVISED

- Regular contact and meetings between the president's administration and members of Congress.
- The Office for Legislative Affairs is a government department which exists to lobby members of Congress to vote for the president's legislation.
- Cabinet ministers and key figures in the president's administration will also reach out to members of Congress, particularly on key votes.
- The administration will 'call in favours' and make deals to secure the votes it needs.
- The executive may subtly modify its legislation to win the support of members of Congress, or offer 'pork' for their home state (see 'pork barrel politics', p. 31).
- The administration will often need votes from across the aisle, so it lobbies representatives from both parties.

Relationship to the Supreme Court
REVISED

- The Supreme Court can rule that Acts of Congress are unconstitutional and therefore no longer law.
- For example, much of the 1996 Defense of Marriage Act (DOMA) was struck down by two Supreme Court rulings: *United States* v *Windsor* (2013) and *Obergefell* v *Hodges* (2015), which effectively legalised same-sex marriage.
- In theory, Congress can overturn the ruling of the Court, but only by passing a constitutional amendment, which would then need to be ratified by the states.
- In practice, the Court's decision usually stands, as it is so difficult to amend the Constitution.
- The Senate plays a key role in the confirmation of Supreme Court justices, determining who ultimately sits on the Court.
- Congress has the power to impeach and try Supreme Court justices.

Exam tip

Although Congress can impeach Supreme Court justices, in reality this is highly unlikely. The last attempt was in 1804, and did not result in a conviction

Now test yourself
TESTED

17 Which two important powers does the Senate possess that the House does not?
18 What is 'pork barrel politics'?
19 Give two reasons why being a senator is generally seen as being a more desirable job than being a congress(wo)man.
20 How can Congress overturn a ruling of the Supreme Court?

Answers on p. 126

Summary

You should now have an understanding of:

- how Congress is structured and its role and powers
- Congress's functions and powers in legislation, oversight and the power of the purse and how effectively it uses these
- the composition of Congress, the different terms of office and party allegiance
- the significance of the party system and the committee system
- the representative role of senators and representatives
- the relative strengths of the House of Representatives and the Senate
- Congress's relationship to both the executive branch of government and the Supreme Court.

Exam practice

1 Explain and analyse three ways in which the committee system may be significant in US politics. [9]
2 Explain and analyse three ways that Congress can check the power of the executive branch. [9]
3 Analyse, evaluate and compare the arguments in the passage below for and against the view that political parties play an important role in Congress. [25]

> Political parties are still the dominant influence in Congress. Parties decide the leadership of both chambers and organise committees and members. As a result, there has always been a clear difference between divided government and united government. In the former scenario, gridlock is more likely than in the latter, when the executive finds it easier to pass bills and receives less oversight from Congress. Furthermore, increasing partisanship and the growing ideological separation between Republicans and Democrats means that party membership is a much better guide to how a member of Congress will vote than it was 30 years ago, when bipartisanship was more common. The number of party unity votes increased from just over 40% in both houses of Congress in 2002 to more than 69% in both houses in 2015.

> However, the 115th Congress (January 2017–present) has shown that the role of the parties can be minimised by other factors. Although the Republicans controlled both houses of Congress, President Trump was unable to repeal Obamacare in his first 100 days, despite promising to do so during his presidential campaign. His bill to repeal and replace Obamacare was subject to intense scrutiny and criticism from members of both parties and was finally defeated by four Republican senators who declared they would vote against it in July 2017. Challenging conventional party leadership, smaller congressional caucuses have become increasingly important, exposing the divisions inside the main two parties. The House Freedom Caucus notably refused to support President Trump's budget in February 2018. It seems that unified government is no guarantee of party unity.

Source: original material written by the another of this book for educational purposes, 2018

Answers and quick quiz online

ONLINE

4 The executive branch of government: president

Article II of the US Constitution gives **executive** power to the **president**.
- The president is indirectly elected via the Electoral College system.
- The president is head of the federal government, head of state and commander-in-chief of the military.
- Executive power is held solely by the president, though he/she may delegate this power to other officials (e.g. members of cabinet).
- The president has a range of powers, only some of which are defined in the Constitution.
- Powers are limited by a system of checks and balances from the legislative and judicial branches of government.
- Different presidents use their powers with varying degrees of effectiveness, leading some observers to worry about an 'imperial presidency', while others have claimed that the presidency is 'imperilled'.

> **Executive** The branch of government in the USA that carries out and enforces laws.
>
> **President** Head of the US government and head of state.

Sources of presidential power

The president's formal powers come from four sources, shown in Table 4.1.

Table 4.1 **Sources of the president's powers**

Source	Type of powers	Explanation	Example
The Constitution	Constitutional powers	• Powers detailed in the Constitution, e.g. the power to propose legislation.	• The president is commander-in-chief of the armed forces, a power given to him by Article II, Section II, Clause I of the Constitution. • President George W. Bush used this power when he led the USA during the Afghanistan and Iraq wars.
Congress	Delegated powers	• Powers given to the president (delegated) by Congress, e.g. the power to determine detailed regulations for Congress's laws	• Congress has delegated the power to impose trade tariffs against a country engaged in 'unfair' trade practices. • In 2018 President Trump announced the introduction of tariffs on steel imports.
Implicit authority from the Constitution or Congress	Implied powers	• The president can claim that the action he is taking is consistent with the authority given to him by the Constitution, or by Congress, even if he has not been given specific authority for it. • For example, the power to use emergency powers if required by circumstances.	• President F.D. Roosevelt used emergency powers to force Japanese-Americans into internment camps during the Second World War.

→

Source	Type of powers	Explanation	Example
The president's constitutional role as head of the executive	Inherent powers	● Not specifically set out in the Constitution but required for the president to carry out his/her role as chief executive. ● The Constitution says 'the executive power shall be vested in a president' and the president should 'take care that the laws be faithfully executed': this provides the justification for inherent powers. ● Unlike implied powers, the justification for specific inherent powers does not link to a specific expressed power, but relates to the fact that they are inherent to the role of president.	● After the 9/11 terror attacks, President George W. Bush argued that his constitutional war powers gave him authority to detain terrorist suspects for an indefinite period and have them transported to other countries for interrogation and torture (a practice known as 'extraordinary rendition').

Exam tip

You need to learn two examples of how different presidents have used the sources of presidential power.

Formal and informal powers

Formal powers

REVISED

Table 4.2 outlines a president's formal powers (the enumerated powers in Article II of the Constitution and the inherent powers of the president).

Table 4.2 **Formal powers of the president**

Executive powers	● Chief executive of the federal government. ● Prepares the annual federal budget, although it must be passed by Congress.
Legislative powers	● Proposes legislation to Congress. ● Signs legislation passed by Congress into law. ● Can choose to veto legislation passed by Congress, to prevent it becoming law (Congress can override a presidential veto, but this is difficult – Congress managed to override only one of Barack Obama's 12 vetoes).
Appointment powers	● Nominates officials to the executive branch, e.g. heads of executive departments, though these must be confirmed by the Senate. ● Nominates all federal judges, including Supreme Court justices when vacancies arise. These must all be confirmed by the Senate.
Foreign affairs powers	● Commander-in-chief of the US military. ● Can initiate military action (e.g. George W. Bush led the USA into wars in Iraq and Afghanistan). ● Negotiates treaties, although these must be ratified by the Senate with a two-thirds super-majority.
Pardons	● The president can pardon someone who has acknowledged that they are guilty of a federal crime.

Informal powers

Table 4.3 outlines a president's informal powers (political rather than constitutional powers).

Table 4.3 Informal powers of the president

'The power to persuade'	● A phrase coined by Professor Richard Neustadt, who argued that persuasion was the most important presidential power. ● The president can use personal influence, the authority of his office and his political capital to convince other key political figures to support him.
Deal-making	● Presidents may win support from politicians by making deals to help them with their own priorities.
Agenda setting	● Because presidents command the spotlight, they set the political agenda. ● All presidents have had this power, but Donald Trump has utilised it more than any other, using Twitter to commandeer the political agenda with controversial tweets and forcing the media to focus on his chosen issues, e.g. immigration, North Korea.
Executive influence	● The president can use the support of his vice president, cabinet officers and his lobbyists in the Office of Legislative Affairs to push forward his agenda.
De facto party leader	● The president is in effect the head of his party, which allows him to influence its membership. ● This is particularly helpful if the president's party controls one or both Houses of Congress, as it should be much easier for him to pass his legislation.
World leader	● The president has huge international influence as the leader of the most powerful superpower in history. ● Most presidents have acted as international leaders, with Ronald Reagan leading the Western powers in the Cold War, George W. Bush leading an international coalition in a 'war against terror' and Barack Obama playing a key role in the 2015 Paris Agreement on climate change. ● Donald Trump has shown less interest in international leadership, announcing a withdrawal from the Paris Agreement, imposing tariffs on imported steel and sending mixed signals about the US commitment to NATO. His negotiations with North Korea suggest that he prefers unilateral action.
Direct authority and stretching of implied powers	● Executive orders can be issued as a form of direct authority. ● President F.D. Roosevelt holds the record, with 3,721 executive orders issued during the Great Depression and the Second World War. ● President George W. Bush used them to authorise controversial anti-terror measures after 9/11, including surveillance of suspects without a court order. ● President Obama continued the trend of relying on executive orders after he became frustrated with Congress's resistance to his agenda and took to issuing executive orders as an alternative to legislation (e.g. increasing the federal minimum wage, outlawing health insurance companies' discrimination against married same-sex couples). ● While a candidate, Donald Trump criticised Obama's use of executive orders. However, by October 2017 President Trump had signed more executive orders than any president in the previous 50 years. ● Under George W. Bush and Barack Obama, signing statements were used increasingly to challenge the constitutionality of aspects of legislation. ● President Trump used a signing statement to criticise a 2017 bill imposing sanctions on Russia, Iran and North Korea, claiming it affected his constitutional powers to conduct foreign policy. ● Executive agreements are used by presidents to avoid the difficult process of getting a treaty ratified by the Senate (a two-thirds super-majority vote is needed). ● Since the Second World War, the number of executive agreements has increased dramatically compared to treaties – from 1977–96, 93% of foreign policy agreements were executive agreements rather than treaties.

→

	• President Obama's use of an executive agreement to commit the USA to the Iran nuclear deal in 2015 frustrated Congress, which argued that it was in effect a treaty and should require Senate approval. • Obama used an executive agreement to commit to the 2015 Paris Agreement on climate change. President Trump is therefore able to withdraw from the agreement without consulting Congress, as he has with the Iran nuclear deal.
Bureaucratic power	• The Executive Office of the President (EXOP) is a collection of offices providing policy advice and administrative and bureaucratic support to the president.

Now test yourself

TESTED

1 What is the name for the formal powers of the president that are not explicitly set out in the Constitution?
2 What is the term for a formal order from the president to the federal government?
3 What are the president's two main foreign policy powers?

Answers on p. 126

Constraints on the president

Table 4.4 outlines the various constraints the president faces.

Table 4.4 **Constraints on the presidency**

Checks and balances by Congress	Effectiveness
Amending, delaying or rejecting the president's legislation	• Without the support of Congress, a president cannot pass legislation, even if public opinion is on his side, e.g. President Obama failed to pass legislation on gun control. • It is less effective during periods of unified government as Congress is less likely to obstruct a president's legislation if a majority of its members are from his party.
Overriding a presidential veto	• This rarely happens, as a two-thirds majority in both houses of Congress is required, e.g. Congress overrode only one of President Obama's 12 vetoes.
Power of the purse	• This is a powerful check on the executive, which needs Congress to pass its budgets. • Congress can extract key concessions from the president in return for passing his budget. • If Congress refuses to pass the president's budget, it can force a government shutdown, putting pressure on the president to agree to its demands.
Refusing to confirm presidential appointments (Senate only)	• This can be very significant, especially with high-profile appointments. • For example, in 2016 the Republicans controlled the Senate and refused to hold confirmation hearings on President Obama's nominee to the Supreme Court, Merrick Garland. The Senate thus prevented the Supreme Court from having a majority of Democrat nominees.
Refusing to ratify treaties (Senate only)	• This occurs rarely – the most significant example was the rejection of the Treaty of Versailles in 1920, which resulted in a much more isolationist US foreign policy in the 1920s. • A two-thirds majority is needed to ratify a treaty: since the Second World War, presidents have increasingly used executive agreements to avoid the ratification process.

The power to declare war	• This is of very limited effectiveness: Congress has not declared war since 1941, despite the USA's subsequent involvement in the Korean, Vietnam, Afghanistan and Iraq wars, though President George W. Bush did receive permission from Congress for military action in Iraq.
Investigation	• High-profile Congressional investigations are an important form of oversight, generating significant media scrutiny. • For example, investigations into the Obama administration's management of the 2012 attack on the US embassy in Benghazi, Libya and investigations into possible collusion between Russia and the Trump campaign in the 2016 presidential election.
Impeachment and trial of the president	• This can ultimately lead to the president being removed from office. • Even if the president is acquitted (e.g. Bill Clinton, 1998), the process of impeachment generates huge media attention and public scrutiny.
Checks and balances by the judiciary	
Judicial review	• Courts can declare the government's actions unconstitutional. • Judicial review may be done by the Supreme Court (e.g. in 2006 President George W. Bush's military commissions for terrorist suspects at Guantanamo Bay were ruled unconstitutional) or by federal courts (e.g. in 2017 President Trump's ban on travellers from certain Muslim-majority countries was halted by federal courts).
Other constraints on the president	
Party support in Congress	• It is more difficult for the president to pass legislation or get nominees confirmed during periods of divided government. • It can be difficult to pass legislation during periods of unified government if the president's party is not united behind him (e.g. President Trump's Republican Party).
The prevailing orientation of the Supreme Court	• Whether the Supreme Court has a conservative or a liberal majority may affect its rulings on government actions and government legislation.
State governors	• State governors can actively work against the president's agenda. • Democrat Californian governor Jerry Brown campaigned against President Trump's decision to withdraw from the 2015 Paris Climate Agreement and signed up California to a separate subnational coalition committed to tackling climate change by reducing greenhouse gas emissions. • State governors' authority is limited to their own state only.
Interest groups	• These may campaign against a president's agenda. • They can be powerful and highly influential, e.g. the National Rifle Association (NRA) successfully motivated Congress and its supporters to resist President Obama's efforts to introduce gun control.
Media	• President Trump repeatedly claims that his agenda is being undermined by 'fake news' generated by liberal-leaning media. • President Obama felt that his administration was unfairly attacked by conservative channel Fox News. • The impact of negative reporting is lessened by the tendency for people to watch a news channel or read a newspaper that supports their pre-existing political leanings.

→

Public opinion	<ul><li>Presidential approval ratings in opinion polls have traditionally been seen as very important.</li><li>The growing partisan divide and reduced number of competitive electoral districts means that presidents may worry less about appealing to the whole nation and can govern with low approval ratings.</li><li>President Trump has the lowest presidential approval ratings in recorded history, with a high of only 46% (as opposed to President Obama's 69% or President George W. Bush's 90% after the 9/11 terror attacks). However, his approval levels with his core supporters remain high.</li></ul>

Typical mistake

Students often assume that all presidents face similar constraints. In fact, political circumstances generally dictate how constrained a president is. President Obama was able to pass legislation with relative ease from 2009 to 2010 as his party, the Democrats, controlled both houses of Congress. This changed when the Republicans won a majority in the House of Representatives in the November 2010 mid-terms. Congress frustrated many of Obama's plans for the rest of his tenure.

Exam tip

If writing about the constraints on the president, be sure to differentiate between the formal checks and balances that can be used against him and the extent to which key variables such as party support in Congress, or the prevailing orientation of the Supreme Court, may affect how those formal checks and balances are applied.

Revision activity

Read through Table 4.4 and work out which you think are the three most powerful constraints on the presidency and which are the three weakest constraints.

Now test yourself

TESTED

4   Which institution needs to ratify presidential nominees and international treaties?
5   Why does the power of Congress to declare war provide only a limited check on the president's power?
6   Why can the orientation of the Supreme Court affect the extent to which it constrains the president?

Answers on p. 126

Relationship between the presidency and other institutions

The president is supported by a number of different institutions.

> **Cabinet** A group of advisers chosen by the president to help him run the federal government. It includes 15 heads of the executive departments (e.g. the secretary of state, the treasury secretary) and may include other advisers.

The cabinet

REVISED

- **Cabinet** members are policy specialists and usually give advice on their specific department rather than giving general political advice.
- The president does not have to take the advice of his cabinet members – the Constitution gives him sole executive authority.

- Cabinet members may be former politicians, academics or experts in their field. Unusually, President Trump appointed several former generals to cabinet positions.
- The cabinet tends to meet a few times a year – the frequency depends on the president's wishes.
- Under President Obama the cabinet met on average 3.5 times a year, compared with 6 times a year under President George W. Bush.
- Cabinet meetings are chaired by the president.

The relationship between the presidency and the cabinet varies, depending largely on the president's attitude to the cabinet:
- President Reagan held many more cabinet meetings than most presidents, suggesting that he valued meeting with his cabinet members in person and hearing their thoughts.
- President Obama rarely met with his cabinet and often used his meetings to brief cabinet members on a significant forthcoming event or policy launch.
- Some individual cabinet members may have a particularly high profile (such as President Obama's secretary of state, Hillary Clinton), or a close political relationship with the president. This can give them greater individual influence with the president than other members.
- President Trump's abrasive style saw him sack secretary of state Rex Tillerson via Twitter in 2018, demonstrating the precarious position of members in his cabinet.

Typical mistake

Students might assume that US cabinet officers enjoy the same status as their UK counterparts. In fact, because of the British system of cabinet government, UK cabinet ministers are part of a collective executive and effectively share power with the prime minister.

The Executive Office of the President (EXOP)

REVISED

The **Executive Office of the President** was set up by President F.D. Roosevelt as the federal government grew during the Great Depression of the 1930s.
- EXOP agencies include the White House Office, the National Security Council, the Office of Management and Budget and the Office of the Vice President.
- There are about 3,000 staff.
- It is headed by the White House chief of staff.

Executive Office of the President A group of about a dozen agencies that supports the president in running the federal government.

The White House Office

REVISED

The White House Office is a collection of important offices that supports the president.
- It includes the Office of the Chief of Staff, the Office of Legislative Affairs, the National Economic Council and the Office of Cabinet Affairs.
- Appointments are at the discretion of the president: they do not need Senate confirmation.
- Many of these offices are based in the West Wing of the White House.
- The White House Office is headed by the **White House chief of staff**, who is responsible for determining who has access to the president.

White House chief of staff The most senior adviser to the president. Heads the EXOP and the White House Office.

The National Security Council (NSC)

The National Security Council is the president's main forum for considering national security or foreign policy issues.

- It is chaired by the president.
- Members include the vice president, secretary of state, secretary of the treasury, secretary of defense. The chairman of the joint chiefs of staff is the military adviser.
- The NSC coordinates national security and foreign policy within the government and all its agencies.

The relationship between the presidency and EXOP varies from one president to another, depending on various factors:

- The relationship between the president and his chief of staff:
  - President Obama worked very closely with Rahm Emanuel, allowing him considerable influence and authority, even over cabinet officers.
  - In contrast, President Trump's first chief of staff, Reince Priebus, resigned after little more than six months.
- The approach the president takes towards his wider staff:
  - President Trump's frequent sacking of officials and the prevalence of resignations by senior staff led to reports of chaos in the White House.
- The extent to which EXOP staff act as political operatives rather than neutral assistants:
  - President George H.W. Bush's chief of staff, John Sununu, was eventually sacked after being criticised for promoting his own conservative policy positions rather than those of the president.
  - President George W. Bush's national security adviser, Stephen Hadley, was so supportive of the president's foreign policy aims that he may not have provided necessary critical analysis.

The federal bureaucracy and federal agencies

Cabinet officers head the various government departments that make up the federal bureaucracy (e.g. the Department of State).

- There are also a large number of independently run federal agencies (e.g. the Central Intelligence Agency (CIA)).
- Some presidents (usually Democrats) aim to increase the scope of the federal bureaucracy, while others (generally Republicans) aim to reduce its size (e.g. in February 2018 President Trump announced plans to abolish 22 government agencies).

Now test yourself

TESTED

7 Which organisation, made up of the heads of the federal departments and other key advisers, does the president chair?
8 Which position is held by the president's most important adviser, who is responsible for EXOP and the White House Office?
9 What is the name of the president's main foreign policy and national security forum?

Answers on p. 126

Revision activity

On an A3 sheet of paper, draw a diagram to show the president and the institutions that support him (cabinet, EXOP, White House Office, White House chief of staff, NSC, federal bureaucracy and agencies). For each one, explain what it does and who is in it. Draw a line from each institution to the president. Along the line, write a description of the relationship between the president and the institution.

Case study: waxing and waning of presidential power

President Barack Obama's two terms illustrate the tendency of power to wax (grow) and wane (shrink) during a single presidency:

- Obama was elected on a wave of optimism in 2008: his presidency was welcomed by millions as a historic triumph for black Americans.
- His presidency was initially helped by Democratic control of both Houses of Congress.
- America faced a serious economic crisis, but Obama had a productive first 100 days and received the highest approval ratings for that period since the 1970s.
- Obama's administration successfully implemented an economic stimulus, support for the financial and automobile industries, environmental reforms and his signature 'Obamacare' health policy (Patient Protection and Affordable Care Act, 2010).
- In November 2010 the Republicans won a majority in the House: from this point on Obama became increasingly frustrated by Congress and divided government.
- Obama won a second term in 2012.
- In 2014 the Senate was lost to the Republicans, so Obama found it even more difficult to advance his political agenda using legislation.
- Obama was loathed by many conservatives, who thought that 'Obamacare' expanded the role of federal government too far into people's lives.
- In an attempt to avoid becoming a **lame duck president**, Obama used executive orders rather than legislation.
- Obama's executive order to protect some illegal immigrants from deportation was challenged by 26 states and declared unconstitutional by the courts.
- His attempt to fill a vacancy on the Supreme Court was blocked by the Senate, which refused to consider his nominee.

> **Revision activity**
>
> Read the case study of Obama's presidency and find evidence for the following reasons why Obama's power waxed and waned: public opinion, Congress, the courts, states, term limit.

> **Lame duck presidency** A period in which the president has lost most of his political power and struggles to implement policy objectives. It typically happens in the latter part of a president's second term, when his influence is limited by the fact that his presidency will soon be ending because of the two-term limit.

Imperial versus imperilled presidency

> **Imperial presidency** Term coined by writer Professor Arthur Schlesinger in 1973 to describe the idea that the modern presidency has an imperial or 'emperor-like' character. Under this model, presidents dominate Congress and conduct foreign policy independently. This type of presidency is unconstitutional as it goes beyond the powers of the president intended by the Founding Fathers.
>
> **Imperilled presidency** In response to the imperial presidency theory, President Gerald Ford (1974–77) argued that the presidency was actually 'imperilled'. Ford claimed that the presidency's effectiveness was limited by an overly assertive Congress and an excessively large federal bureaucracy.

Does the USA have an imperial or an imperilled presidency?

Table 4.5 gives points to suggest the USA has an **imperial presidency** and then points to suggest an **imperilled presidency**.

Table 4.5 An imperial presidency or an imperilled presidency?

Imperial	Imperilled
● Schlesinger's argument was based on the presidency of Richard Nixon (1969–74), who authorised military intervention in Cambodia and Laos without telling Congress. ● The 1972 Watergate scandal showed that Nixon was using corrupt and illegal methods to advance his own interests. ● Nixon continued the war in Vietnam without congressional approval, even after Congress had revoked the Tonkin Gulf Resolution in 1971 (this had originally been passed in 1964, giving the president congressional authority to take any military action in Vietnam). ● Most modern presidents have taken military action without congressional approval – Congress has not formally declared war since 1941. ● The use of executive orders, signing statements and executive agreements as a means to rule using direct authority shows presidents' willingness to push their powers to their constitutional limits. ● The size and scope of the federal bureaucracy has continued to increase since the 1970s, at the behest of presidents. ● President Ronald Reagan (1981–89) had a much more imperial style than presidents Carter and Ford, particularly in foreign policy, where he led the West to victory at the end of the Cold War. ● The 9/11 terrorist attacks on America resulted in President George W. Bush increasing presidential power by announcing a 'war on terror', invading Afghanistan and Iraq and detaining terrorist suspects without trial at the Guantanamo Bay detention centre. ● President Obama did not close Guantanamo Bay and his unmanned drone programme allowed him to launch ten times more air strikes in the Middle East and Asia than his predecessor. ● Obama did not seek congressional approval for his 2011 military intervention in Libya, despite the War Powers Act (1973). ● Donald Trump's presidency has arguably been more imperial in style than any previous presidency, with his use of executive orders, and willingness to conduct foreign policy and sack advisers via Twitter. ● In January 2018 President Trump's lawyers argued in a memo that as the president had authority over all federal investigations, he could not be made to testify to special counsel Robert Mueller's investigation into the 2016 election campaign. In June 2018 Trump tweeted that he had an 'absolute right' to pardon himself, effectively claiming impunity from the law.	● Congress responded to Nixon's presidency by passing new laws restricting the powers of the president – the 1973 War Powers Act was designed to stop presidents from ordering military action without congressional approval. ● Gerald Ford argued that the federal bureaucracy's size made it difficult for presidents to ensure their wishes were properly carried out. ● Gridlock, particularly during periods of divided government, makes it very difficult for presidents to pass their legislation. ● Government shutdowns demonstrate the weakness of the presidency. ● The use of executive orders and direct authority is generally an expression of weakness rather than strength – presidents use these methods as a lesser alternative to legislation when they lack the support of Congress. ● President Obama's weakness was evident when the Senate refused to discuss his nominee for the Supreme Court in 2016. ● Presidents including Reagan, G.W. Bush and Trump have blamed Congress for forcing them to sign budgets that would increase the size of the deficit. ● Every two-term presidency is imperilled to some extent towards the end of the second term, when the president effectively becomes a lame duck. ● President Trump's presidency has been weakened by historically low approval ratings, regular firing of senior White House staff and cabinet officers, failure to command reliable support from a Republican-majority House and Senate, and the impression of chaos and lack of a coherent policy. ● Divisions within the Republican Party have prevented President Trump from relying on his own party's support in Congress. Despite having a united government, Trump faced a brief government shutdown in February 2018 because of the objections of Republican Senator Rand Paul to the budget.

Now test yourself

TESTED ☐

10 Which presidency generated claims of an 'imperial presidency'?
11 Why was Obama's presidency weakened after 2010?
12 What evidence is there that President Trump has engaged in nepotism (promoting one's family or friends)?

Answers on p. 126

Summary

You should now have an understanding of:

- the president as the head of the executive and that the Constitution gives him sole executive power
- the president's range of formal and informal powers, but that these powers are limited by checks and balances from Congress and the courts
- the president being supported by his cabinet, the Executive Office of the President (EXOP), the White House Office and the federal bureaucracy and agencies
- how presidential power may wax and wane during a presidency
- the debate as to how far the presidency is 'imperial' or 'imperilled'.

Exam practice

1 Explain and analyse three sources of formal presidential power. [9]
2 Explain and analyse three ways in which the presidency has been weakened in recent years. [9]
3 Analyse, evaluate and compare the arguments in the passage below for and against the view that the system of checks and balances is an effective constraint on the president. [25]

> The system of checks and balances provides an impressive range of constraints upon the power of the president. Congress scrutinises and may reject government legislation, demonstrating its independence even during periods of united government. It is able to check the president's spending using the 'power of the purse' and the Senate's approval is needed to confirm presidential appointments. The Supreme Court prevents the president from acting unconstitutionally and Congress can remove him from office for improper conduct.
>
> However, there are limits to the effectiveness of these checks and balances. Presidents have found ways to overcome their constraints, using direct authority to bypass Congress, particularly during periods of national emergency, and engaging in multiple military conflicts without asking for a congressional declaration of war. Congress has rarely been able to find the votes to override a presidential veto. More often than not, political factors constrain the president more effectively than constitutional ones.

Source: original material written by the author of this book for educational purposes, 2018

Answers and quick quiz online

ONLINE ☐

5 Comparing the US and UK executives

The chief executive of the US government is the president and in the UK it is the prime minister.
- Both leaders have very different roles and powers as a result of structural differences in the two systems of government.
- The prime minister is part of the legislature, the president is not.

> **Exam tip**
>
> The essay questions on the AQA US Politics exam paper are comparative, meaning that they ask you to compare an aspect of US politics or government with an aspect of UK politics or government. Be sure to revisit your notes from each course as the examiners are looking for specific examples from each country. The examples in this chapter are suggestions of how the executives compare, but they are not the only possible answers.

Roles and powers of the UK prime minister and of the US president

Table 5.1 outlines the roles and powers of the leaders of the UK and the USA.

Table 5.1 **Roles and powers: the UK prime minister versus the US president**

Roles and powers	Similarities	Differences
Chief executive	• Both are head of government.	• The president is a singular executive, as explained in Article II of the Constitution. • Under the system of cabinet government, the prime minister is *primus inter parus* (first among equals) in a collective executive. • The president has greater executive power than the prime minister, e.g. executive orders, executive agreements, signing statements.
Head of state		• The president is also the head of state. • In the UK, this role is performed by the monarch.
Legislation	• Both can initiate legislation.	• Congress develops its own programme of legislation, whereas in Parliament a government programme of legislation receives the vast majority of time. • In the USA the government can suggest legislation to Congress, but it may be rejected. • If the prime minister's party has a majority in the House of Commons, they can use their position as leader, patronage – including offering government jobs to MPs – and the whip system to ensure the government's legislation is passed. • The president has less ability to influence Congress to pass his legislation: the separation of powers makes party discipline much weaker and his powers of patronage are more limited as he cannot offer government jobs to members of the legislature. • Only the president can veto legislation.
Financial powers		• The president is dependent on congressional approval for his budget. On occasion, government shutdowns mark a failure in negotiation. • In the UK government shutdowns do not occur because it is relatively simple for the government to pass budgets through Parliament, as it usually has a majority.

Roles and powers	Similarities	Differences
Military powers	● Both act as the key military decision-maker. ● In practice, presidents frequently order military action without consulting Congress, as UK prime ministers can without consulting Parliament.	● The president is commander-in-chief of the armed forces, whereas in the UK the monarch performs this role. ● In theory, the president cannot declare war, whereas in the UK the prime minister can do so using the royal prerogative (though there is an increasing tendency for UK prime ministers to seek Parliament's approval).
Appointments		● The president's appointments to cabinet and executive branch positions require Senate confirmation, whereas the UK prime minister can appoint whomever they choose. ● The US president nominates Supreme Court justices and federal judges. These also need Senate approval but give the president a degree of influence over the judiciary that the UK prime minister lacks.
Election		● Unlike the UK prime minister, the US president is directly elected, so has a direct personal mandate from the people. ● In contrast, the UK prime minister is the leader of whichever political party has enough support in the House of Commons to form a government.
Term limits		● The prime minister has no term limits, whereas the president cannot serve for more than two full terms.
Succession	● The president appoints a vice president. ● The prime minister may choose to appoint a deputy if they wish.	● The vice president will undoubtedly succeed the president if he dies, retires or is removed from office. ● The prime minister will be succeeded by whomever leads the party with most support in the House of Commons, following either an internal leadership election or a general election. This has not been the deputy prime minister since 1955.
Patronage	● Both can reward supporters with cabinet or government positions.	● The power of patronage is more useful to the prime minister, as they can offer government jobs to MPs in return for their support. ● MPs who are members of the government are known as the payroll vote because the prime minister can depend on their loyalty. ● The separation of powers prevents the president from influencing members of Congress in this way. ● The prime minister can also recommend supporters for **life peerages** or **honours**.
Pardon		● The power of pardon is held by the president. ● In Britain the monarch can issue a royal pardon on the advice of the justice secretary.

Life peerage Gives the recipient a title (e.g. Baron William Hague) and a seat in the House of Lords for the duration of their lifetime.

Honours Give the recipients a medal and either a knighthood or admission to a different 'order of chivalry', e.g. MBE = Member of the Most Excellent Order of the British Empire.

Now test yourself

TESTED ☐

1 Which leader must be a member of their country's legislature?
2 Which leader is commander-in-chief of their country's military?
3 Which leader has the most developed powers of patronage?

Answers on p. 126

Accountability to the legislatures

Table 5.2 looks at the similarities and differences in accountability.

Table 5.2 Accountability: similarities and differences

	Similarities	Differences
Passing legislation	● Both leaders introduce their legislative agenda for the year to their legislatures – the president makes a State of the Union address to Congress and the monarch delivers the Queen's Speech on behalf of the prime minister. ● During periods of minority government, the prime minister may also struggle to get their legislation through Parliament. ● Both budgets are scrutinised by the legislatures.	● The president generally finds it more difficult to pass his legislation through Congress, particularly during periods of divided government. ● Prime ministers are usually able to rely on their parliamentary majority. ● Presidents are much more likely to see their budgets defeated in Congress, potentially resulting in government shutdown. ● Prime ministers can use the whip system to ensure party discipline, whereas presidents have to make deals and convince members of Congress to support them.
Scrutiny of the executive	● Both legislatures use the committee system to scrutinise the actions of their government.	● The prime minister appears in the House of Commons every week to face MPs' questions at Prime Minister's Question Time and also speaks in key debates in the Commons.
Removal from office		● The House of Commons can call a vote of no confidence in the government: a simple majority vote is enough to remove the prime minister and their government from office. ● The president can be removed only after impeachment by the House of Representatives and conviction by the Senate – a much more complex process.

4 Which leader usually finds it more difficult to pass their legislation through the legislature?
5 Which event in Parliament does the UK prime minister attend every week, allowing MPs to question him/her directly?
6 Which legislature can remove the head of government most easily?

Answers on p. 126

Relationship to other institutions of government

Table 5.3 looks at the similarities and differences in relationship to other institutions of government.

Table 5.3 Other institutions of government: similarities and differences

	Similarities	Differences
Cabinet	• US cabinet officers are generally responsible for a specific government department, as are UK cabinet ministers. The prime minister and the president both select the members of their cabinets.	• The president's cabinet nominees need Senate confirmation. • The prime minister is *primus inter parus* in a system of collective cabinet government, whereas the president does not share executive authority with his cabinet officers. • US cabinet officers are responsible for running their own government department only – unlike the UK there is no doctrine of collective responsibility. • UK cabinet ministers are often the prime minister's political rivals (e.g. formes Foreign Secretary Boris Johnson was probably appointed to the cabinet to prevent him from challenging Theresa May), whereas US cabinet officers are not rivals of the president. • UK prime ministers use regular cabinet reshuffles as a form of patronage and control. • The US cabinet is not used to further the president's control of his party in this way. • Cabinet government means that the prime minister can fall from power if they lose the support of their cabinet (as happened to Margaret Thatcher). • The US cabinet cannot threaten the president's position.
Executive administration	• Both leaders require administrative support.	• EXOP is much more extensive than the Prime Minister's Office and the Cabinet Office.
Wider bureaucracy	• Both leaders act as chief executive for the government bureaucracy – the federal government and agencies in the USA, and the UK civil service and government agencies.	• The vast majority of top officials in the UK civil service do not change from one government to the next. • In contrast, a new US government administration needs to fill around 4,000 government positions, more than a quarter of which require Senate confirmation.

Now test yourself

TESTED ☐

7 Which leader governs as part of a collective executive?
8 Which leader holds cabinet meetings most frequently?
9 Which leader has the most extensive administrative support?

Answers on p. 126

Theoretical approaches to the executives

Table 5.4 considers approaches to the executives.

Table 5.4 Theoretical approaches to the executives

	Aspects to analyse
Structural The role of political institutions	• Difference between parliamentary and presidential government: the prime minister *must* be a member of Parliament, whereas the separation of powers means that the president *cannot* be a member of Congress. • Difference between a singular executive and cabinet government. • Contrast between the administrative support provided to prime ministers and presidents. • Differences in the scope of their role: the president is commander-in-chief and head of state, unlike the prime minister. • Different processes for removal from office result in increased job security for the US president. • The separation of powers gives the president far less ability to enforce his will on Parliament than a prime minister with a majority.

Rational
 	
The role of individuals
	• Different individuals have approached the presidency in different ways. For example:
	  • President Trump has favoured an aggressive 'imperial' style towards government, firing members of his cabinet and government by Twitter and using executive orders frequently. He has also left hundreds of key government positions unfilled more than a year after taking office.
	  • President Obama increasingly favoured unilateral action, using executive orders and executive agreements to avoid asking for congressional approval, and rarely calling cabinet meetings.
	  • Presidents Ford and Carter were seen as weak and ineffective occupants of an 'imperilled presidency'.
	• Different individuals have approached the role of prime minister in different ways. For example:
	  • Tony Blair was accused of a 'presidential' style of government in which he overlooked his cabinet.
	  • David Cameron was highly focused on his cabinet, particularly the Quad committee of himself, his chancellor of the exchequer and the two most senior Liberal Democrats in his coalition government.

Cultural The role of shared ideas and culture	• US political culture affords the president a degree of respect that the UK prime minister does not receive. • The doctrine of collective cabinet responsibility creates a culture of cabinet government in which prime ministers are criticised if they appear to be exceeding their 'first among equals' status.

Now test yourself

TESTED

10 Which of the three theoretical approaches best explains the differences between the president and the prime minister?
11 Which prime minister was accused of a 'presidential' style of government?
12 What parliamentary factor tends to affect the prime minister's attitude to their cabinet?

Answers on p. 126

Summary

You should now have an understanding of:
- how, as chief executive, head of state and commander-in-chief, the president has a broader role than the prime minister, who is simply the head of the government
- prime ministers being 'first among equals' in a system of cabinet government – their success is partly determined by their ability to use cabinet effectively to further their objectives
- how the president embodies a singular executive, but the separation of powers means that his ability to influence Congress is limited
- how, provided the prime minister has a majority and strong party discipline, they will find it easier to pass legislation than a president does.

Exam practice

1 Explain and analyse three ways in which structural theory could be used to study executive/legislative relations in the USA and the UK. [9]
2 'Prime ministers and presidents are equally constrained by their ability to influence their legislatures.' Analyse and evaluate this statement. [25]
3 'The constitutional power of the prime minister exceeds the power of the president.' Analyse and evaluate this statement. [25]

Answers and quick quiz online

ONLINE

6 The judicial branch of government

The judicial branch of government is the system of courts that interpret and apply the law.

- The **Supreme Court** is the highest court in the USA, the final court of appeal for anyone seeking justice.
- Its power of **judicial review** allows it to rule on whether laws, or the actions of government, are constitutional.
- The Supreme Court interprets the Constitution – some justices interpret it strictly according to what its framers intended, others have a looser approach.

Overview: the Supreme Court

The Supreme Court is the highest court in the federal judiciary.

- It has nine **justices**: an odd number so that decisions are not tied.
- There is one chief justice (John Roberts) and eight associate justices.
- Justices are appointed by the president and confirmed by the Senate.
- Justices hold office for life unless they retire or are impeached and found guilty.
- The Supreme Court hears only cases of constitutional importance.
- Cases are appealed from the US District Courts to US Courts of Appeals and then to the Supreme Court.
- The Supreme Court's power of judicial review allows it to rule on Acts of Congress or state laws, or federal or state executive actions, and decide whether they are constitutional or not.

The process of selection and appointment of Supreme Court judges

The process is as follows:

- Vacancy opens: as a result of the death, retirement or impeachment of a sitting justice.
- President considers possible nominees: suggestions are made by his advisers, his party and legal experts.
  - Most nominees come from the federal Courts of Appeals: at the time of writing, eight out of nine justices came from the Courts of Appeals.
  - Presidents need to be confident that their candidate will attract the necessary support in the Senate to be confirmed.
- Candidates are shortlisted and background-checked.
- A final few are interviewed by the president.
- The president's choice is formally announced, resulting in massive media attention.
- Nominee appears before the Senate Judiciary Committee – witnesses help the committee assess the nominee's suitability.

Supreme Court The highest court in the USA. It is the final court of appeal for the USA and is responsible for interpreting the Constitution.

Judicial review The power of the Supreme Court to decide whether a law or action is unconstitutional.

Justices Judges who sit on the Supreme Court. There are nine and they have life tenure.

Typical mistake

All justices must hear each case, but there are not always nine justices ruling. If a seat on the Court is empty, or if a justice has been recused (excused because they have a connection to the case in question), the Court can try cases with fewer members, provided that there are at least six. There were eight justices on the Court after associate justice Antonin Scalia's death in 2016, until Neil Gorsuch was appointed in 2017. If the Supreme Court is tied (e.g. 4–4), the lower court's decision stands.

- Senate Judiciary Committee votes on the nominee – this is a recommendation to the Senate.
- Senate debates and votes on the nominee. A simple majority is needed for confirmation. Defeat at this stage is relatively rare (see Figure 6.1).

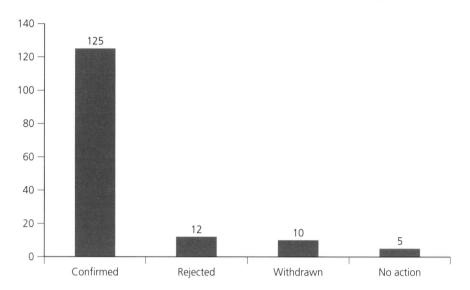

Figure 6.1 Result of Supreme Court nominations, 1789–2017

Table 6.1 considers the strengths and weaknesses of the process.

Table 6.1 Nomination of Supreme Court judges: strengths and weaknesses

Strengths	Weaknesses
<ul><li>Detailed scrutiny of every nominee by the White House, the FBI, the Senate Judiciary Committee and the media – any past misdemeanour or controversial decision will probably be uncovered.</li><li>Several opportunities for unsuitable candidates to be withdrawn from the process.</li><li>The Senate Judiciary Committee undertakes detailed scrutiny of the candidates.</li><li>Senate confirmation provides an important check on the power of the president – he must choose a candidate who will command sufficient support from senators.</li><li>Attempts by presidents to pick justices who share their political philosophy are not always successful – Republican President G.H.W. Bush appointed Justice David Souter in 1990, but Souter was an unexpectedly liberal member of the court.</li></ul>	<ul><li>Presidents usually try to choose nominees who appear to support their own political philosophy.</li><li>The Senate Judiciary Committee appears to be politicised – questioning from the opposition party is often aggressive or focused on embarrassing the nominee rather than on analysing judicial expertise.</li><li>Questioning from the president's party is generally much softer, leading to fears that if the Senate is held by the president's party, it will carry out little effective scrutiny.</li><li>Voting by the Senate generally takes place on party lines, suggesting politicisation.</li><li>The Senate's refusal even to consider Merrick Garland (President Obama's nominee) in 2016 was in effect a violation of the president's right to appoint a justice to the Court.</li><li>In April 2017 Republicans removed the requirement for Supreme Court nominees to pass a 50-vote threshold in the Senate. Nominees are now confirmed by a simple majority vote. A President whose party also controls the Senate therefore does not need to pick a nominee with bipartisan appeal.</li><li>The politicisation of the process is increased by pressure group campaigns for or against nominees.</li><li>Media interest in nominees can be intrusive and may focus on their personal life or politics.</li><li>When Brett Kavanaugh faced accusations of sexual assault during his confirmation process in 2018, he was publicly defended by President Trump, who ridiculed his accuser. The Senate's decision to confirm Kavanaugh has damaged many Americans' faith in the integrity of the Court.</li></ul>

Current composition of the Supreme Court

Table 6.2 shows the composition of the Supreme Court at the time of writing.

Table 6.2 Supreme Court membership, 2018

Justice	Date appointed	President appointing
Chief Justice		
John Roberts	2005	George W. Bush (R)
Associate Justices		
Clarence Thomas	1991	George H.W. Bush (R)
Ruth Bader Ginsburg	1993	Bill Clinton (D)
Stephen Breyer	1994	Bill Clinton (D)
Samuel Alito	2006	George W. Bush (R)
Sonia Sotomayor	2009	Barack Obama (D)
Elena Kagan	2010	Barack Obama (D)
Neil Gorsuch	2017	Donald Trump (R)
Brett Kavanaugh	2018	Donald Trump (R)

- The Court has five Republican-appointed justices (John Roberts, Clarence Thomas, Samuel Alito, Neil Gorsuch and Brett Kavanaugh) and four Democrat-appointed justices (Ruth Bader Ginsburg, Stephen Breyer, Sonia Sotomayor and Elena Kagan).
- Roberts, Thomas, Alito, Gorsuch and Kavanaugh are seen as the conservative wing of the Court – they tend to reach judgements that conservatives support.
- Ginsburg, Breyer, Sotomayor and Kagan are seen as the liberal wing of the Court – they tend to reach liberal judgements.
- Anthony Kennedy was known as the 'swing vote' on the Court – he made conservative judgements on issues such as gun control and campaign finance, but made liberal judgements on abortion, LGBT rights and affirmative action. Following Kennedy's retirement in July 2018, President Trump nominated Brett Kavanaugh to replace him. As a result, the Court now has a 5-4 conservative majority.
- Clarence Thomas is the only African-American on the Court and the second in its history (the first was Thurgood Marshall in 1967).
- There are three women on the Court: Ginsburg, Sotomayor and Kagan (the first was Sandra Day O'Connor in 1981). Only four women have sat on the Court.
- Sonia Sotomayor is the first and only Hispanic justice on the Court.

Now test yourself

TESTED ☐

1 How many seats are there on the Supreme Court?
2 Which committee scrutinises nominees to the Supreme Court?
3 Which House of Congress confirms presidential nominees to the Supreme Court?
4 Why was Merrick Garland, President Obama's 2016 nominee to the Court, not appointed?

Answers on p. 126

> **Typical mistake**
>
> Do not assume that the presence on the Court of broadly conservative and broadly liberal justices means that judgements are always divided along those lines. In fact, the Court regularly reaches unanimous judgements (more than 50% of judgements from 2016 to 2017), suggesting that the political leanings of the justices are less important than their shared legal expertise.

The nature of judicial power

The Supreme Court has the power of judicial review, which allows it to declare:

- ○ Acts of Congress unconstitutional
- ○ actions of the executive unconstitutional
- ○ actions of the state governments, or Acts passed by state legislatures, unconstitutional.
- This ensures that all branches of federal and state government are complying with the Constitution.
- The Constitution was written in 1787, so it is not always clear how it applies to modern situations – the Court therefore plays a crucial role in interpreting what the Constitution means.

The constitutional role of the Supreme Court

Supreme Court as the guardian of the Constitution/constitutional interpretation

REVISED

- The Court makes its judgements based on its interpretation of what the Constitution means.
- Supreme Court justices have very different ideas about how the Constitution should be interpreted.
- **Strict constructionists** believe that the text of the Constitution should be followed as closely as possible.
- **Loose constructionists** believe that the Constitution should be interpreted more loosely, taking account of the general intentions of the framers and the modern context.
- Strict constructionists are usually appointed by Republican presidents and at the time of writing include Chief Justice John Roberts and associate justices Clarence Thomas, Samuel Alito, Neil Gorsuch and Brett Kavanaugh.
- Loose constructionists are usually appointed by Democrat presidents and currently include associate justices Ruth Bader Ginsburg, Stephen Breyer, Sonia Sotomayor and Elena Kagan.

> **Exam tip**
>
> It is generally more helpful to analyse the role of strict and loose constructionists on the Court than it is to focus on 'conservative' or 'liberal' justices. This is because the former terms explain how justices approach their role of interpreting the Constitution, which is the basis of their judgements.

> **Strict constructionism**
> The legal philosophy that the Constitution should be interpreted strictly according to what it actually says and what its framers originally intended. Strict constructionists are usually conservatives.
>
> **Loose constructionism**
> The legal philosophy that the Constitution should be interpreted loosely by applying the general intentions of its framers to a modern context. Loose constructionists are usually liberals and believe that the Constitution is a living constitution, which can be interpreted to suit the changing needs of society over time. They focus on context rather than on language.

Supreme Court as protector of citizens' rights

REVISED

The Supreme Court protects civil rights and liberties. The Bill of Rights is interpreted and protected by the Court.

Examples of how the Court has interpreted the Bill of Rights in recent years are given in Table 6.3.

Table 6.3 Supreme Court interpretation of the Bill of Rights

First Amendment: freedom of religion *Congress shall make no law respecting an establishment of religion, or prohibiting the free exercise thereof.*	• The Court needs to strike a balance between avoiding an 'established' religion (one adopted by the state) and allowing citizens to practise their religion freely. • The trend over the past few decades appears to be allowing individuals more freedom to practise their religion. • 1960s–90s: the Court ruled against Christian practices in state-run schools because the 'establishment of religion' is forbidden in the Constitution. • In *Zelman* v *Simmons-Harris* (2002), the Court upheld a school voucher programme in Ohio, which gave government aid to parents so that they could send their children to private schools, the vast majority of which were religious. • In *Town of Greece* v *Galloway* (2014), the Court ruled that prayers at the start of council meetings did not constitute 'an establishment of religion' and therefore could continue.
First Amendment: freedom of speech *Congress shall make no law… abridging the freedom of speech, or of the press.*	• Political donations are seen as an expression of free speech and have been protected by the Court. • In *Buckley* v *Valeo* (1976), the Court ruled that limits on spending by presidential candidates were unconstitutional. • In *McConnell* v *Federal Election Commission* (2004), the Court ruled that banning unrestricted 'soft money' donations to political parties (money from individuals or corporations that is given to a political party rather than to a candidate and that can be spent on anything) was constitutional. • In *Citizens United* v *Federal Election Commission* (2010), the Court controversially ruled that corporations, unions and associations had the same rights to free speech as individuals and could make political donations and political adverts. • In *McCutcheon* v *Federal Election Commission* (2014), the Court ruled against a limit on total political donations.
Second Amendment: gun control *A well-regulated Militia, being necessary to the security of a free State, the right of the people to keep and bear Arms, shall not be infringed.*	• Liberals interpret the amendment as conferring a collective right to bear arms in a militia (a military force made up of civilians, used in the US War of Independence, 1775–83). • Conservatives usually claim that the amendment provides an individual right to bear arms. • In *District of Columbia* v *Heller* (2008), the Court ruled that the amendment does confer an individual right to bear arms. • Any future attempt by state or federal government to ban gun ownership would therefore require an amendment to the Constitution.
Eighth Amendment: the death penalty *Excessive bail shall not be required, nor excessive fines imposed, nor cruel and unusual punishments inflicted.*	• The death penalty is legal in 31 US states. • Supreme Court rulings have focused on interpreting what constitutes 'cruel and unusual punishment'. • In *Roper* v *Simmons* (2005), the Court ruled against the death penalty for crimes committed by a minor (a person under the age of 18). • In *Baze* v *Rees* (2008), the Court ruled that lethal injection was not 'cruel and unusual punishment' and could therefore be used for executions.

Revision activity

For each of the cases in Table 6.3, decide whether the verdict reached would have been favoured by liberals or conservatives.

Now test yourself

TESTED ☐

5 What term describes justices who believe that the Constitution should be interpreted according to the original intentions of the framers?
6 What term describes justices who believe that the Constitution should be interpreted according to the modern needs of society?
7 For which amendment has the Supreme Court needed to define the meaning of 'cruel and unusual punishment'?
8 Which amendment forms the basis of Supreme Court rulings on political donations?

Answers on p. 126

The significance of judicial review

Judicial review allows the Supreme Court to ensure that the legislature and the executive do not exceed their constitutional powers.

● Judicial review allows the Supreme Court to strike down laws passed by legislatures (Congress or state legislatures) if it finds them to be at odds with the Constitution.
● The Supreme Court can also rule against the actions of the government (federal or state).
● Judicial review can be used as a check on presidential power, as in the judgement *Boumediene* v *Bush* (2008), which ruled that foreign nationals detained at Guantanamo Bay by President G.W. Bush's administration had a right to challenge their detentions in federal courts, and *United States* v *Texas* (2016), which struck down President Obama's executive order that around 5 million illegal immigrants be given an indefinite delay in deportation.
● Judicial review ensures that the civil rights and liberties of ordinary Americans are not infringed by executives or legislatures.
● It gives nine unelected justices enormous power over elected federal and state legislatures and executives.

Debates about the political significance of the Supreme Court

The Court has often been criticised for making political decisions.

● Decisions such as *Roe* v *Wade* (1973), which stated that women had a constitutional right to an abortion, or *Obergefell* v *Hodges* (2015), which ruled that it was unconstitutional to prevent same-sex marriage, have the same effect as a new law legalising abortion or same-sex marriage.
● Critics have labelled the Court a 'quasi-legislative' body, arguing that it has moved beyond interpreting the law, to making it.
● Strict constructionists argue that the framers had no intention of authorising abortion or same-sex marriage when they wrote the Constitution. They claim these rulings are an example of judicial activism and 'legislating from the bench'.
● Many justices prefer to practise judicial restraint, in which they uphold the principle of *stare decisis* and rarely overturn legal precedent.

Is the Supreme Court too political?

Table 6.4 outlines the arguments for and against the Supreme Court being too political.

Table 6.4 Supreme Court: is it too political?

Yes	No
<ul><li>It is an unelected body but makes decisions on important matters of public policy.</li><li>Justices are appointed by the president and confirmed by the Senate, in a highly politicised process.</li><li>Most justices broadly reflect the political stance of the president who appointed them.</li><li>Most justices tend to make either broadly conservative or broadly liberal judgements.</li><li>Loose constructionist approaches to interpreting the Constitution have led to criticisms of the Court acting as a 'third house of the legislature' – in effect, making rather than interpreting law.</li><li>Justices who believe in a living constitution are able to use their position for judicial activism, making decisions that they believe improve society but which were not intended by the framers (e.g. same-sex marriage).</li><li>The Court makes decisions on the most politically controversial areas of US public policy, e.g. abortion, affirmative action, gun control, marriage rights and immigration.</li><li>In its notorious *Bush* v *Gore* (2000) decision, the Court ruled that a recount in Florida was unconstitutional. One of the most controversial decisions made by the Court, it decided the result of the 2000 general election, with George W. Bush becoming president as a result.</li></ul>	<ul><li>Justices are independent and are supposed to be politically neutral.</li><li>Decisions are made on the basis of legal argument rather than political principles.</li><li>Some justices do not reflect the political stance of the president who appointed them, e.g. David Souter.</li><li>Some justices do not consistently vote the same way, e.g. Anthony Kennedy was a 'swing vote'.</li><li>Many justices are strict constructionists, who practise judicial restraint.</li><li>If the Constitution is to continue to be relevant, the Court must apply it to modern areas of public policy, even if this is controversial.</li><li>Congress acts as a check on an overly political Supreme Court – if it wished to, it could initiate a constitutional amendment to overturn the Court's decision.</li></ul>

Now test yourself

9 What is the term for the power used by the Supreme Court to rule on the constitutionality of laws or executive actions?

10 What term describes an approach to judgements that aims to produce positive change in society?

11 What term describes an approach to judgements that avoids dramatic change and favours deferring to the elected branches of government?

12 Who acted as the 'swing vote' on the Court until his retirement in 2018?

Answers on p. 126

Two examples of landmark rulings and related debates and controversies

There are two particular landmark rulings that have led to controversy (see Table 6.5).

Table 6.5 **Supreme Court: landmark rulings**

	Case details	Significance
Brown v *Board of Education of Topeka* (1954)	<ul><li>13 African-American parents from Topeka, Kansas, brought this lawsuit after their children were denied access to their local all-white school, forcing them to travel miles to attend an all-black school.</li><li>The parents were supported by the National Association for the Advancement of Colored People (NAACP) and represented by the lawyer Thurgood Marshall (who later became the first African-American Supreme Court justice).</li><li>The Supreme Court ruled unanimously in favour of the parents, finding that the doctrine of '**separate but equal**' facilities was fundamentally unequal and a breach of the Fourteenth Amendment, as citizens have the right to 'equal protection' under a state's laws.</li></ul>	<ul><li>In *Plessy* v *Ferguson* (1896), the Court had ruled that 'separate but equal' provision was constitutional; in *Brown* v *Board of Education of Topeka* it broke with precedent and reversed its decision.</li><li>Chief Justice Earl Warren explained that even if 'tangible' aspects of education were equal, the 'intangible' result of **segregation** was a feeling of inferiority and reduced educational attainment.</li><li>In a follow-up judgement in 1955, the Court ordered local school authorities to integrate public schools.</li><li>The judgement was a huge boost to the growing civil rights movement and to the NAACP.</li><li>The decision ended more than half a century of legal segregation.</li><li>In the South, where segregation was most entrenched, the decision was seen as an attack on states' rights by the federal Supreme Court.</li><li>This led to a confrontation at Little Rock, Arkansas, in 1957, when the state governor supported the high school's decision not to admit nine African-American students. President Eisenhower eventually ordered federal troops to escort them into the school.</li><li>The judgement can be seen as the product of an activist court: justices broke with precedent and Warren worked hard to ensure a unanimous verdict was reached (as any division would make criticism of the judgement easier).</li></ul>
Obergefell v *Hodges* (2015)	<ul><li>This case also focused on the 'equal protection' clause of the Fourteenth Amendment.</li><li>James Obergefell argued that in refusing to recognise his same-sex marriage (performed in Maryland), the state of Ohio was in breach of the Fourteenth Amendment.</li><li>The Court ruled 5–4 in favour, with the majority arguing that the right to marry was a fundamental right, supported by the equal protection clause.</li></ul>	<ul><li>The judgement legalised same-sex marriage across the USA (previously it was legal in 36 states).</li><li>It was a victory for loose constructionist justices, who interpreted the Constitution according to the modern context.</li><li>For the minority of strict constructionists on the Court, the judgement was an example of judicial activism and 'legislating from the bench' rather than interpreting the Constitution according to its original meaning.</li><li>Many Christian groups were horrified, with some arguing that their right to religious freedom was being infringed (a view also shared by the dissenting justices).</li><li>A hugely significant change was made to US law, by an unelected body.</li></ul>

Separate but equal A doctrine established by the Supreme Court in *Plessy* v *Ferguson* (1896) that 'separate but equal' facilities for whites and African-Americans were constitutional. In reality, facilities were often not equal, as white facilities tended to receive better funding. The idea of racial inferiority was legitimised, as was segregation.

Segregation In the South, state legislatures passed segregation laws (known as Jim Crow laws) after *Plessy* v *Ferguson* which enforced separate facilities for whites and African-Americans. These included separate parks, schools, restrooms, water fountains, restaurants and public transport.

> **Revision activity**
>
> Read the two case studies in Table 6.5 and make a note of the similarities and differences between them.

> **Exam tip**
>
> The syllabus asks for two case studies that establish a new legal concept or principle, changing the interpretation of existing law. Make sure you can explain how *Brown* v *Board of Education of Topeka* and *Obergefell* v *Hodges* represented a change in the law and why this was significant.

Significance of the judiciary in shaping one area of public policy: abortion

The topic of abortion has been contentious (see Table 6.6).

Table 6.6 **Abortion: case studies**

Case	Details	Significance
Roe v *Wade* (1973)	• Using the name 'Jane Roe', a woman named Norma McCorvey challenged the right of Texas law to prevent her from having an abortion. • The Court ruled 7–2 that women did have the right to an abortion in the early stages of pregnancy, as part of the 'liberty' protected by the Fourteenth Amendment.	• This was a landmark case for the women's movement, asserting a woman's right to personal choice regarding her body. • Abortion became a defining political issue, with most Democrats identifying as 'pro-choice' and most Republicans and evangelical Christians as 'pro-life'. • The case was seen as an example of unelected justices 'legislating from the bench', as the ruling had the same effect as passing a law to legalise abortion. • Some argued that a law passed by Congress would have proved broader support and a democratic mandate for abortion rights.
Planned Parenthood v *Casey* (1992)	• The Court upheld the right of states to regulate abortion in the early stages of pregnancy, provided that this regulation was not an 'undue burden' on a woman seeking an abortion.	• The Court had a conservative majority, leading some to hope that *Roe* v *Wade* would be overturned. • The Court applied *stare decisis* by protecting the right to an abortion defined in *Roe* v *Wade*. • However, the states had increased power to regulate abortion, provided that they met the 'undue burden' test.

Case	Details	Significance
Gonzales v *Carhart* (2007)	• The Partial-Birth Abortion Ban Act (2003) was passed by Congress and signed into law by President George W. Bush. • The Act was ruled unconstitutional in the lower federal courts. • The Court ruled 5–4 in favour of the Act.	• 'Partial-birth' abortions in later pregnancy remained illegal, as intended by Congress. • The Court allowed Congress to ban this type of abortion, even if the woman's health was affected (though not if her life was in danger). • Inspired by their success, religious and conservative pressure groups switched to a strategy of gradually reducing abortion rights through legislation and legal challenges, rather than overturning *Roe* v *Wade*. • The identity of the judges may have played a role – Ginsburg was the only woman on the Court and opposed the decision. The five justices in the majority were all Catholic. Moderate justice Sandra Day O'Connor had retired and been replaced by Samuel Alito, who was more conservative.
Whole Woman's Health v *Hellerstedt* (2016)	• The Court ruled 5–3 that restrictions placed on abortion clinics by Texas state law were unconstitutional as they placed an 'undue burden' on women.	• This was a setback for the conservative strategy of using legislation to reduce access to abortions. • Associate Justice Anthony Kennedy provided the crucial swing vote.

Following Brett Kavanaugh's appointment to the Court in 2018 the 5–4 conservative majority may result in future judgements that erode abortion rights further.

Revision activity

Read through Table 6.6 and find examples of the following:
• judicial activism
• judicial restraint
• loose constructionism.

Exam tip

If asked whether the Supreme Court has too much power, you should consider how it uses judicial review to check the actions of the federal and state governments and strike down laws. One argument is that the Court provides an important check and balance on the other two branches of government, but you should also evaluate the view that it is prone to judicial activism and 'legislating from the bench'.

Now test yourself

TESTED ☐

13 Which doctrine of racial segregation did *Brown* v *Board of Education of Topeka* overturn?
14 What did the Court legalise in *Obergefell* v *Hodges*?
15 Which famous judgement legalised abortion in the USA?
16 How have subsequent Supreme Court judgements modified abortion law?

Answers on p. 126

Summary

You should now have an understanding of:
- how the nine justices on the Supreme Court are appointed by the president and confirmed by the Senate, in a highly politicised process
- the fact that justices sit on the Court for life, unless they retire or are removed by impeachment
- some justices being strict constructionists, others being loose constructionists who believe in a 'living Constitution'
- the Court's power of judicial review, which allows it to strike down laws passed by federal or state legislatures and to rule that actions of federal or state executives are unconstitutional
- the important role the Court plays in protecting civil rights and liberties
- the Court's judgements on controversial areas of public policy, which have made it politically very significant.

Exam practice

1 Explain and analyse three ways in which the Supreme Court has protected civil rights. [9]
2 Explain and analyse three ways in which the Supreme Court interprets the Constitution. [9]
3 Analyse, evaluate and compare the arguments in the passage below for and against the view that the Supreme Court is a political institution. [25]

The Supreme Court has been a political institution ever since its landmark judgement *Marbury* v *Madison* (1803), the first time it struck down an Act of Congress as unconstitutional. Since then it has not shied away from controversy, ruling on important areas of public policy including civil rights, affirmative action and immigration, and even determining the outcome of the presidential election in *Bush* v *Gore* (2000). The Supreme Court took it upon itself to declare that abortion was legal in 1973 and in 2015 pronounced that the right to same-sex marriage was also protected by the Constitution. It is the *de facto* third house of the legislature and surely the most powerful.

However, many of the justices are strict constructionists, who favour judicial restraint. Despite being political appointees, they do not always vote according to the politics of the president who appointed them. While it is possible to divide the justices into liberals and conservatives, the fact that the Court regularly returns unanimous verdicts demonstrates that judges are assessing each case on its legal merits rather than making simplistic political decisions. All the justices are legal experts, who take their job of interpreting the Constitution very seriously. That some consider it to be a 'living Constitution', requiring interpretation to apply it to a modern context, does not mean their judgements are inherently political. The process of amending the Constitution is so complex that a modern interpretation is surely helpful to ensure it stays relevant.

Source: original material written by the author of this book for educational purposes, 2018

Answers and quick quiz online

ONLINE

7 Comparing the US and UK judiciaries

There are many similarities between the US and the UK judiciaries.
- The US judiciary is headed by the US Supreme Court.
- The UK judiciary is headed by the UK Supreme Court.
- The UK Supreme Court is a much newer creation, dating from 2009.
- Both play a significant role in interpreting the nation's laws.
- Both act as a check on the power of the executive by reviewing the actions of the government.
- However, the US Supreme Court is more powerful than the UK one.

Exam tip

Comparative exam questions will expect you to have a detailed knowledge of both the US and the UK judiciaries, so make sure you revisit your notes and work through the key concepts and terminology for each.

Similarities and differences between the supreme courts

The US and UK supreme courts are separate from the other branches of government (see Table 7.1).

Table 7.1 US and UK supreme courts: similarities and differences

	Similarities	Differences
History	• Both supreme courts were designed to provide an independent judiciary, fully separate from the other two branches of government.	• The US Supreme Court was included in the original Constitution and first met in 1790. • The UK Supreme Court was created in 2009, so it is still a new institution. • Prior to 2009 the Law Lords sat in the Appellate Committee of the House of Lords.
Selection and appointment of justices	• Both systems involve detailed scrutiny of potential candidates.	• US justices are nominated by the president and confirmed by the Senate in a highly politicised process. • UK justices are chosen by an independent selection commission and then presented to the Lord Chancellor (a government minister) for approval, in a process which receives much less media attention than the appointment of justices in the USA. • There are no official requirements to be a US Supreme Court justice, whereas UK Supreme Court justices must have been either a senior judge for at least 2 years or a senior courts lawyer for 15 years.
Characteristics of justices	• Justices in both the USA and the UK are experienced legal practitioners – either judges in a lower court or practising lawyers. • Women and ethnic minorities are under-represented on both courts, relative to their percentage of the population.	• There is a slightly higher proportion of women on the Supreme Court (3 of 9 justices in 2018, compared with 3 of 12 justices in the UK). However, the president of the UK Supreme Court is a woman, Lady Hale. • There are no ethnic minorities on the UK Supreme Court, whereas two of the nine US justices are from ethnic minorities. • The different proportions of women and ethnic minorities are partly explained by the higher proportion of both groups in the lower courts of the USA (the main recruitment pool for justices) compared with the UK.

→

	Similarities	Differences
Tenure of justices	● Both UK and US Supreme Court justices enjoy security of tenure.	● UK justices must retire by age 75. ● US justices have life tenure (unless they choose to retire or are impeached and removed from office).
Judicial approach	● Some justices in the USA practise judicial restraint (*stare decisis*, judicial deference), which is much closer to the approach followed by UK justices.	● Loose constructionism and the idea of a 'living Constitution' are judicial principles that do not apply in the UK, where the interpretative role of judges is more limited than it is in the USA.

Typical mistake

Do not assume that because the Law Lords sat in Parliament prior to 2009 as the Appellate Committee of the House of Lords, they were not independent. In fact, the Law Lords operated with much the same degree of independence as today's Supreme Court, which was created to provide a formal separation of powers.

Revision activity

Consider the differences between the two supreme courts and decide which are the most significant and least significant.

Impact on government and politics

Table 7.2 outlines the impact of the two courts.

Table 7.2 US and UK supreme courts: impact

Similarities between the two supreme courts	Differences between the two supreme courts
● Both have made controversial rulings declaring the government's actions unlawful. ● Both have ruled against laws passed by the legislature.	● The UK Supreme Court's impact is less as the government can pass **retrospective legislation** to legalise its actions after the Supreme Court has ruled against it, whereas in the USA the Court's judgement can be overruled only by a constitutional amendment. ● The US Supreme Court has a much bigger impact as it can strike down laws, whereas in the UK, Parliament remains sovereign and so has the final say on whether its legislation stands. ● The US Supreme Court has made important judgements on public policy which have had a dramatic impact, e.g. legalising abortion (*Roe* v *Wade* 1973) and same-sex marriage (*Obergefell* v *Hodges* 2015) and the historic abolition of the 'separate but equal' doctrine (*Brown* v *Board of Education of Topeka* 1954), which led to the end of racial segregation. ● The UK Supreme Court has not made judgements of the same magnitude because the sovereignty of Parliament prevents the Court from 'legislating from the bench'. ● The UK Supreme Court is still a very young institution – its impact may evolve over time.

Now test yourself TESTED ☐

1 Which Supreme Court justices have life tenure?
2 Which Supreme Court justices are nominated and appointed by politicians?
3 Which Supreme Court has had the greater impact on government and politics?

Answers on p. 127

Retrospective legislation A law that legalises something that occurred before the law was passed.

Extent and bases of powers

> **Typical mistake**
>
> Although both supreme courts have the power of judicial review, they are not equally powerful. The US Supreme Court's verdict can be overridden only by constitutional amendment, whereas the UK Supreme Court can be overridden by a simple majority vote in Parliament (see Table 7.3).

Table 7.3 US and UK supreme courts: similarities and differences

	Similarities between the two supreme courts	Differences between the two supreme courts
Extent of powers	● Both are final courts of appeal for those seeking justice (with the exception of EU law in the UK, for which the final court of appeal is the European Court of Justice). ● Both courts can use judicial review to consider the actions of the government – an important check on the power of the executive. ● Both courts can rule against the actions of the government: the US Supreme Court can find them unconstitutional, the UK Supreme Court can rule them to be *ultra vires*.	● In the UK, Parliament is sovereign, so the Supreme Court cannot strike down Parliament's laws, whereas the US Supreme Court can strike down an Act of Congress. ● The US Supreme Court can rule against laws or government actions that contravene the Bill of Rights, whereas the UK Supreme Court can only identify a law or action as being incompatible with the European Convention on Human Rights (ECHR) (much of which is incorporated into the UK Constitution as the Human Rights Act (1998)) and invite Parliament to consider redrafting legislation. ● Parliament can ignore the UK Supreme Court's 'declaration of incompatibility' or simply pass a new law to overrule it. ● The US Supreme Court's verdicts can be overruled only by a constitutional amendment. ● The US Supreme Court can make 'interpretative amendments' to the Constitution. ● The UK Supreme Court cannot amend the Constitution (though it can clarify its meaning). ● UK governments can use their control of Parliament to pass retrospective legislation to authorise actions which the Supreme Court has ruled *ultra vires*, whereas US governments are unable to override their court's ruling.
Bases of powers	● Both have the power to interpret the meaning of their constitutions and make judgements accordingly.	● As the UK does not have a codified constitution, the interpretative power of its Supreme Court is less significant than in the USA and focuses mainly on interpreting the Human Rights Act (and, prior to Brexit, European Union law). The UK Supreme Court also reviews legal precedent (previous law made by judges) and decides how it applies to new cases. In contrast, the US Supreme Court is concerned with the wording in a single document, the Constitution. ● The US Supreme Court derives its authority from Article III of the Constitution, which gives it 'the judicial power of the United States', whereas the UK Supreme Court was created by an Act of Parliament. ● The UK Supreme Court's powers were given to it by Parliament, whereas the US Supreme Court's power of judicial review is not mentioned in the Constitution and derives from its own actions – it independently overrode an Act of Congress in *Marbury* v *Madison* (1803) and has enjoyed the power of judicial review ever since.

Relative independence of the US and UK judiciaries

The evidence suggests that both the US and the UK judiciaries enjoy a high degree of **judicial independence**:

- Their position is protected from government interference as they have life tenure (US justices) or tenure until age 75 (UK justices).
- Since the creation of the UK Supreme Court in 2009, both judiciaries have been structurally and physically independent from the other two branches of government.
- Both judiciaries have made judgements against the ruling government, e.g. *United States* v *Texas* (2016), which struck down President Obama's executive order giving millions of illegal immigrants an indefinite delay in deportation, and *R (on the application of the Public Law Project)* v *Lord Chancellor* (2016), which ruled that the Lord Chancellor was acting *ultra vires* by imposing a residence test for legal aid (state support with legal costs).
- US judges may vote against the political interests of the politicians who appointed them, e.g. in *Clinton* v *Jones* (1997), associate justices Ruth Bader Ginsburg and Stephen Breyer judged that President Clinton's office did not make him immune to prosecution, despite both having been appointed by him to the Court.
- US Supreme Court justices are viewed as 'liberal' or 'conservative' in a way that UK justices are not, but the large proportion of unanimous judgements in the US Supreme Court suggests that their legal decisions are not dominated by their political stance.

> **Judicial independence** The idea that judges are free from external pressure, improper influence or interference when making their decisions. They should therefore be able to make decisions based solely on the law.

However, there are also concerns that public criticism is causing **politicisation** of the two judiciaries:

- Both have received hostile public criticism of their judgements, leading to fears that their independence might be affected:
  - President Trump has repeatedly attacked the US judiciary and US Supreme Court, tweeting furiously about 'so-called judges' in 2017 and the 'broken and unfair' court system in 2018.
  - President Obama criticised the Supreme Court's *Citizens United* v *Federal Election Commission* (2010) judgement in his 2010 State of the Union address.
  - In 2016 the UK's *Daily Mail* ran a front-page headline labelling High Court judges 'Enemies of the People'. This was in response to their ruling that the government could not trigger Article 50 in order to leave the European Union.
  - In 2013 Home Secretary Theresa May accused judges of 'ignoring' deportation law by interpreting the Human Rights Act in a way that made it more difficult to deport foreign criminals.
- In 2017 the UK's Lord Chief Justice said that social media 'abuse' put judges under 'intolerable pressure'.
- Although politicians in both countries have occasionally spoken out against their judiciaries for political decisions, President Trump's sustained criticism of the judiciary is unprecedented.

> **Judicial politicisation** A situation in which judges are drawn into politics, compromising their neutrality as guardians of the law. Politicisation may occur because of their own judgements or because of criticism from high-profile sources, e.g. politicians and the media. It represents a threat to judicial independence, particularly if judges feel pressured to make certain judgements to avoid negative publicity.

Typical mistake

Students can confuse judicial independence with judicial neutrality, though they are not quite the same. Judicial neutrality means that judges should be neutral when judging cases, making decisions based on the law and not on their personal opinions. In effect, it describes their internal state when making decisions. Judicial independence means that judges should be free of external influences when making decisions.

Now test yourself

TESTED

4 Which Supreme Court can only have its judgements overridden by a constitutional amendment?
5 Which term is used by the UK courts to indicate that a government official is acting 'beyond their powers'?
6 Give a recent example of extreme political criticism of the US Supreme Court.
7 Give a recent example of extreme public criticism of the UK Supreme Court.

Answers on p. 127

Exam tip

In a question about judicial independence, remember that public criticism of the judiciary from high-profile sources can affect judicial independence. Judges could feel under pressure not to make judgements that will attract condemnation. Driven partly by social media, the changing political culture has certainly seen an increase in hostile criticism of the judiciary in recent years.

Theoretical approaches to the judiciaries

Table 7.4 considers the structural, rational and cultural differences between the US and the UK judiciaries.

Table 7.4 The US and UK judiciaries: theoretical approaches

	Aspects to analyse
Structural The role of political institutions	• A codified US Constitution results in a more powerful and potentially activist judiciary than in the UK. • Parliamentary sovereignty in the UK results in a less powerful Supreme Court, as it cannot override Parliament. • Similarities in tenure allow judicial independence.
Rational The role of individuals	• There are individual differences between justices, their voting preferences and degree of politicisation. • Judicial activist justices are present on the US Court. • The role of President Trump in undermining judicial independence.
Cultural The role of shared ideas and culture	• Contrast the reverence traditionally shown to the US Supreme Court by the political culture of the USA with the low public profile of the new UK Supreme Court. • Creation of the UK Supreme Court was part of an attempt to modernise the UK Constitution and to make the judiciary more accessible to the public. • Both courts exist in cultures that prize the rule of law and judicial independence. • There are competing cultures of judicial restraint and judicial activism in the US judiciary, along with conservative and liberal judicial approaches. • In the UK, criticism by politicians and media about 'liberal' judges has focused on judgements relating to the Human Rights Act, suggesting a cultural difference between the judiciary and the people's elected representatives in Parliament. The *Daily Mail*'s 'Enemies of the People' headline suggested a perceived cultural battle between liberal judges and the democratic will of the people.

Now test yourself

TESTED

8 Which theoretical approach would be best used to analyse the differences in the powers given to the two supreme courts by their constitutions?
9 Which theoretical approach is helpful in analysing the divisions between liberal and conservative attitudes to the judiciaries?

Answers on p. 127

Summary

You should now have an understanding of:
- how the US Supreme Court enjoys greater power than its UK equivalent, as it can strike down laws and rule executive actions unconstitutional and can be overridden only by constitutional amendment
- the UK Supreme Court being less powerful as it can be easily overridden by Parliament, which is sovereign
- how the US Supreme Court has had the most significant impact on government and politics, making dramatic changes to public policy in civil rights, abortion and same-sex marriage
- how, as political appointees, US Supreme Court justices are perceived as conservative or liberal in a way that UK justices are not, though this does not necessarily affect their independence
- how, in recent years, public criticism of both judiciaries has become both more widespread and more aggressive, leading to fears that their independence may be compromised
- the three theoretical approaches – structural, rational and cultural theory – which can be used to analyse the two judiciaries.

Exam practice

1 Explain and analyse three ways in which cultural theory could be used to study the impact of the US and UK supreme courts. [9]
2 'The US Supreme Court can better hold the government to account than its UK equivalent.' Analyse and evaluate this statement. [25]
3 'Citizens' rights are better protected by the judiciary in the USA than in the UK.' Analyse and evaluate this statement. [25]

Answers and quick quiz online

ONLINE

8 The electoral process and direct democracy

Key terms and concepts

Key distinctive features of US elections and voting behaviour include:

- Primaries and caucuses – the methods used to select candidates for elected office. Most prominent are the presidential primaries and caucuses, but they are also used to choose candidates for Congress. Primaries involve a formal secret vote, while caucuses are more informal party gatherings that select delegates who in turn choose the candidate.
- National nominating conventions – held by each party in the summer of the presidential election year to formally elect their presidential candidate. In recent times, these are more a 'coronation' and media opportunity.
- Direct democracy – in the USA this comprises ballot initiatives, recall elections and referendums. Note that different states have different arrangements and there is no provision for a nationwide referendum as in the UK (e.g. the 2016 Brexit vote).
- Voting behaviour – why US citizens vote the way they do. Many factors are also applicable to the UK (e.g. wealth and age), but in the USA, religion and race are especially significant.
- Low levels of turnout/abstention – America, despite a huge number of opportunities to vote, has considerably lower turnouts compared with other western democracies.
- Incumbency – the high levels of re-election usually enjoyed by existing senators and House members. This is often a result of both **gerrymandering** (for House elections) and the political advantages enjoyed by incumbents, such as name recognition and superior fundraising.

> **Gerrymandering** The deliberate manipulation of House district boundaries for political advantage, often leading to some oddly configured House districts. It often leads to major distortions between the popular vote and number of House districts won. For example, in North Carolina in 2016, the Republicans won just 53% of the popular vote but 77% of the House seats.

The electoral system and timing of US elections

The electoral system used throughout the US is **majoritarian** – this helps explains two-party dominance.

- There are elections for president every four years, for all 435 members of the House of Representatives every two years, while a third of the Senate is elected every two years on a rolling basis. For a quick reminder of exactly how Congress is elected, see p. 23.
- Congressional elections occurring between those for president are known as mid-terms and often provide a useful indication of how popular/unpopular a president is. This function is partly served by local elections in the UK.
- The election for president is indirect and done via the **Electoral College**. Each state (plus Washington DC) receives an allocation of Electoral College votes (ECVs) equivalent to the size of its congressional delegation. Thus every state has a minimum of three ECVs (all states have at least two senators and one House member). California has the largest number (55), equating to its two senators

> **Majoritarian** An electoral system where the candidate with the most votes overall wins the race. Also known as first past the post.

> **Electoral College** The indirect electoral system used to elect the US president every four years. Each state (plus Washington DC) is allocated a number of votes depending on population. There are 538 college voters and a simple majority (270) is needed to win. Occasionally, as in 2016, the winner may lose the popular vote nationwide but still win the Electoral College vote and become president.

and 53 House members. Washington DC has no voting members of Congress but the Twenty-First Amendment (1961) gave it three ECVs.

- Reflecting its federal nature, the organisation of elections is the responsibility of each state, though local election laws must comply with federal laws (e.g. Voting Rights Act) and the Constitution. This means there is some variation between states over voter ID laws, primaries and the use of direct democracy.

Main characteristics of US presidential and congressional campaigns

Frequency

American politics is often described as involving 'constant campaigning' due to the sheer number and frequency of elections.

- National elections occur every two years but involve not only congressional elections (and presidential elections every four years) but also those for state governments, governor and other local offices, including some judges.

Focus

REVISED

US elections are more dominated by personalities, not least because candidates are largely responsible for their own fundraising and policy platform.

- Much election advertising and publicity material does not even mention the candidate's party.
- 'All politics is local' according to former House Speaker Tip O'Neill. Many elections, especially for Congress, focus on local issues and what the candidate promises (or has delivered) to benefit the local area, such as federal funds for transportation projects.
- Increasingly, and especially for the presidential elections, the focus is also on the party and its national platform/policies.
- Although much of the focus is on persuading voters to change allegiances, equally important often is 'getting out the vote'. Natural or potential supporters who stay at home can often cost an election.

> **Exam tip**
>
> There is a good opportunity here for a synoptic link with the Constitution. Biennial congressional elections set out by the Constitution often lead to divided government where Congress and White House are controlled by different parties. This makes it even harder to pass legislation.

Format

REVISED

Campaigns involve extensive (and expensive) use of both old and new media.

- The three televised TV debates between the presidential candidates remain central features of the campaign. However, they are perhaps increasingly less influential nowadays as voters are more partisan and so less willing to switch their vote.
- Much of the campaign involves promoting a candidate's character. Regular religious practice, stable family background, a successful business record and being an armed services veteran are among virtues regularly trotted out.

- The other side of the coin involves denigrating one's opponents via **attack ads**. Marital infidelities, corrupt business dealings, avoiding military service and being inattentive to voters' wishes are among the regular insults thrown at opponents, including from one's own party during primaries.
- For a number of reasons (see below), US elections are very expensive. The total cost of the 2016 election was around $6.5 billion.
- Last-minute events or revelations in the presidential election, known as **October surprises**, can also prove important in determining the outcome.

Candidate selection and nomination

Candidate selection works very differently in the USA compared with the UK, with greater opportunity for voter involvement and a much reduced role for the national party.

Exam tip

The election of Donald Trump as Republican candidate is an example of the weakness of the national party leadership over candidate selection. He was an outsider candidate strongly opposed by many of the party establishment, and won because of the support of ordinary Republican voters who participated in primaries and caucuses.

Primaries

REVISED ☐

Tables 8.1 and 8.2 outline the main features of primaries and caucuses.

Table 8.1 Primaries – advantages and drawbacks

Definition	Categories	Key examples	Advantages	Drawbacks
A secret ballot to select each party's candidate. Used in over two-thirds of states, including the biggest and most urbanised.	Open – voters can choose on the day which party's primary to vote in. Closed – voters can participate only in the primary of the party with which they are registered. Non-partisan blanket/jungle (congressional elections only) – there are no party primaries, just a single vote to select the top two candidates who go forward to the general election.	New Hampshire – first primary in the season. South Carolina – 'first in the South'. Alabama – open primary. New York – closed primary. California – non-partisan/jungle primary.	Allows ordinary voters to choose their party's candidate. Preferable to 'smoke-filled' rooms where party bosses traditionally made these choices. Tests candidates' qualities for the office, e.g. fundraising, media presence, stamina and grasp of policy issues. Staggered length of primary campaigns enables a wide range of states to influence the outcome, especially as larger states tend to vote later.	Adds to the overall cost and length of campaigns. Increases the focus on candidates rather than party or policies. Open primaries can encourage voters to opt for the weakest candidate for the opposition party – 'raiding'. Jungle primaries can result in two candidates from the same party being selected, e.g. the 2016 California Senate election was between two Democrats.

Caucuses

Table 8.2 Caucuses – advantages and drawbacks

Definition	Key examples	Advantages	Drawbacks
An informal series of party meetings which ultimately select delegates for the national nominating convention. Voting is open, not secret, and each caucus can last several hours. Used in a minority of states, mainly more rural and less populated ones.	Iowa – first caucus of the season.	Enables more thorough discussion and debate among party activists of candidates' strengths and weaknesses. No opportunity for 'raiding' as in primaries.	Length and timing often discourage many voters from participating, especially those involved in shift work, or who are housebound or have childcare responsibilities. No secret ballot. Attracts mainly strong party activists/more ideological and extreme voters.

National nominating conventions

The conventions are held by each party after primary/caucus elections in the summer, before the presidential election in November.

● They formally nominate the party's candidate. Hence election is more a 'coronation'.
● They are often characterised by plenty of balloons, celebrities (Meryl Streep – Democrats in 2016) and interesting headwear. Television coverage of conventions often shows delegates wearing hats featuring the party symbols of elephants, donkeys and much else besides.
● They are important in terms of media coverage and presenting a united front after a divisive primary campaign (for example, Sanders and Clinton in 2016).
● They are often held in 'swing states' – for example, in 2016 the Republican convention was in Cleveland, Ohio, and the Democrats held theirs in Philadelphia, Pennsylvania.
● The convention provides a chance for the candidate to put forward their vision/priorities and to energise the party faithful.
● In theory, the convention could be politically important in candidate selection if there is no clear winner from the primaries, leading to a 'brokered convention'.
● A successful convention often leads to a short-term boost in poll ratings and greater momentum for the candidate: the 'big mo'. For example, both Trump and Clinton received a short-term boost in the polls of around 4% after their respective conventions.

> **Typical mistake**
>
> Do not assume that conventions are purely political theatre. They do still fulfil an important role in US politics.

The debate over the Electoral College

Workings of the Electoral College

The various features of the Electoral College are as follows:

● It is used only to elect the president.
● It is an indirect form of election based on 538 voters selected by each state (and Washington DC).

- The number of Electoral College votes is calculated by the size of each state's congressional delegation, i.e. senators and House members combined.
- Nearly all states use a 'winner-takes-all' format, i.e. the winning candidate takes all the ECVs for that state regardless of the margin of victory. As in 2000 and 2016, this can distort the final result as the winning candidates lost the popular vote but secured more ECVs because of how their vote was distributed.
- Maine and Nebraska use a slightly different system to allocate their ECVs. Two ECVs go to the overall winner, and one ECV is allocated to the winning candidate in each district. In Maine in 2016, Clinton won three ECVs and Trump one ECV.
- A simple majority is needed for victory. In the event of a tie/no candidate getting a majority, the House of Representatives chooses the president (the Senate chooses the vice president). This last happened in 1824.

> **Exam tip**
>
> If evaluating the Electoral College, it can be a good idea to distinguish between reform and abolition. Potential reforms could include sanctions again faithless voters and awarding electoral votes proportionally.

Controversy over the Electoral College

REVISED ☐

The Electoral College has often been criticised, especially when it delivers the 'wrong result', as in 2000 and 2016 (see Table 8.3).

Table 8.3 Criticisms of the Electoral College

Arguments against the Electoral College	Arguments for the Electoral College
Winner of the popular vote can fail to be elected president, e.g. 2016 and 2000.	Normally delivers the 'right' result, e.g. 2008 and 2012.
Smaller states are over-represented, e.g. California has one electoral vote per 712,000 people, while Wyoming has one electoral vote per 195,000 people.	Reflects the federal nature of the USA and ensures candidates campaign in a range of states, not simply the most populated.
Drawn up by the Founding Fathers in a very different era politically, e.g. before the age of mass communications, gender and racial equality, etc., when direct elections were viewed with suspicion and the USA was much smaller and less diverse.	No superior method has gained widespread and bipartisan support. All the alternatives have their own problems.
Encourages candidates to focus on 'swing states', such as Florida, rather than states 'safe' for one party, e.g. New York.	A nationwide popular vote would lead candidates to focus on large urban areas. 'Go hunting where the ducks are' (Barry Goldwater) still applies.
Faithless electors who, despite being pledged to vote for one candidate, decide to vote for another – a record seven in 2016.	Faithless electors have never affected the final election outcome. Also, the issue can be remedied by passing laws requiring electors to vote for their pledged candidate.
Depresses turnout, especially in safe states, as most states use 'winner takes all' to choose their electors.	Laws could be passed to award electors proportionally in each state without the need to abolish the Electoral College, which would require a constitutional amendment.
Public opinion: polls suggest a majority of Americans want to replace the Electoral College with a direct popular vote – 54–41% 2016.	Much of the support for reform comes from 'bad losers' and peaks after 'rogue results'. Most Americans would prioritise other political reforms, e.g. campaign finance.
Discriminates against independents/third parties, 'wasted vote' syndrome.	Produces a clear winner – the presidency cannot be shared out proportionally.

What factors affect the outcome of US elections?

Many of the factors that explain the outcome of US elections are the same as those in the UK, such as voter profile, but a few such as incumbency are more relevant to the USA.

Money

REVISED

As a general rule, higher-spending candidates have a greater chance of winning elections.

- Incumbents traditionally outspend challengers. In the 2016 Senate elections, on average, incumbents raised $8.7 million while challengers raised just under $600,000.
- Money is spent on a whole range of campaigning activity, including private polls and social media. The bulk of it continues to be spent on television advertisements though.
- Money is no guarantee of success. Hillary Clinton raised and spent more than Donald Trump in 2016 but lost the election.
- A lot of the money spent on advertising is producing material that attacks other candidates – 'attack ads'.

Media

REVISED

The media, both old and new, play an important role in US election campaigns.

- Closely tied in with money (see above), candidates desire positive and frequent media coverage.
- Traditionally, the three televised presidential debates were seen as especially important. This is less true nowadays when there are fewer truly independent voters willing to be swayed. Also, more voters get their political news and information from social media and other internet sources.
- The media are traditionally important in raising the profile and name recognition of candidates. This might have been important in 2008 with the then little-known Obama and in 2012 with Republican candidate Mitt Romney. It was arguably irrelevant in 2016, as both main candidates were very well known to voters.
- The media focus on the two main parties and their candidates and this is often cited as a reason why third parties/independents fare badly.
- Increasingly, candidates spend and concentrate on the new media – it is estimated that together, Trump and Clinton in 2016 spent $81 million on Facebook ads.
- Much of the broadcast media is already informally politically aligned, e.g. Fox News is predominantly watched by Republicans and MSNBC by Democrats. This limits the importance of the old media in changing political views. The same largely applies to the new media. Few Democrats probably follow leading Republicans on Twitter and vice versa for Republicans following prominent Democrats. This again limits the ability of the media to change voting behaviour; it is perhaps more important today for reinforcing political allegiances and encouraging turnout.

> **Exam tip**
>
> Again the 2016 election is a good example of the declining influence and relevance of the TV debates. Most polls suggested Clinton won all three debates (a view shared by a margin of 52–39% in one poll after the final debate), yet this appeared to have minimal impact on the final result.

Issues

REVISED

Despite strong pre-existing political partisanship, issues and policies shape the vote of many Americans, above all independent or undecided voters.

- Issues encompass a mixture of past achievements/failures, especially for incumbents, and future policy pledges.
- At different times, different issues dominate – for example, in 2004, the main issue was probably security and foreign policy after the 9/11 attacks. The economy is normally very important though – former president Bill Clinton was largely correct to comment, 'It's the economy, stupid.'
- Key issues in 2016 included immigration and the personal qualities (or lack thereof) of both main candidates.
- Candidates are normally keen to prioritise and get media coverage on issues about which they feel strongest and to downplay policy areas where they might appear vulnerable.

Leadership

REVISED

Especially at presidential level, leadership qualities play a big role in campaigns and voting outcomes.

- Much of this comes down to trust, perceived competency and general 'likeability'.
- Great emphasis is placed on both personal integrity and ability to cope in a crisis.
- The qualities expected are arguably somewhat contradictory and elusive to find in a single individual. For example, presidents in a crisis are expected to be calm and clear-headed yet also consultative and displaying a sense of urgency.
- Leadership is closely tied in to candidate personalities and track records. Past indiscretions such as affairs or business failures are often highlighted by opponents as rendering a candidate unworthy of the 'highest office in the land'.

Significance of incumbency

REVISED

Incumbents have an advantage in all US elections and enjoy high re-election rates. In 2016, 93% of senators and 98% of House members were re-elected.

- However, high re-election rates should not be taken as evidence for wider popular approval of the political institutions themselves. Congress as a whole has had positive approval ratings of barely more than 10% in recent years. This paradox is perhaps best explained by Americans blaming other states' congress(wo)men, not their own.
- Since 1945, only three US presidents have failed to be re-elected: Ford in 1976, Carter in 1980 and George Bush Senior in 1992. By contrast, eight have been re-elected, most recently Obama in 2012.
- Incumbents tend to do better since they raise and spend more money, they have greater name recognition and they have established campaign teams and staff. They can also highlight concrete past achievements and voting records to electors. There was also the issue of 'pork barrelling', namely getting federal money channelled into often dubious but expensive local projects, e.g. the 'Bridge to Nowhere' in Gravina Island, Alaska.
- House representatives can be helped by friendly gerrymandering, though a hostile one can equally jeopardise re-election even for a long-serving incumbent.

Typical mistake

Traditional pork barrelling is more of a historic problem as the policy, known as 'earmarks', was ended in 2011 by Congress.

Now test yourself**   TESTED

1. Who are the three US presidents since 1945 not to have been re-elected?
2. What was the key issue in the 2004 election?
3. Which party's voters are most likely to watch Fox News?
4. Where are increasing amounts of campaign funds being spent?
5. Which candidate raised the most money in 2016?

Answers on p. 127

Debate over campaign finance

American elections of all types are becoming increasingly expensive. The 2016 election saw presidential and congressional candidates spend around $6.5 billion, of which around $2.4 billion went on the presidential race and just over $4 billion on congressional contests.

Why is the cost of US elections so high?   REVISED

There are various reasons for the high cost of elections.

- The sheer number and frequency of elections has resulted in money being spent not only on presidential and congressional races but also on campaigning in primaries, state government elections and ballot initiatives.
- Efforts to restrict campaign expenditure, such as the 2002 Bipartisan Campaign Reform Act (McCain–Feingold Act), have been largely ineffective. This is due both to loopholes in the Act and to Supreme Court decisions (see below).
- The First Amendment guarantees free speech and this has been extended to a high level of freedom regarding the ability to raise and spend funds for election campaigns.
- Supreme Court decisions, most notably the 2010 Citizens United case, have weakened laws passed by Congress. Citizens United allowed corporations, pressure groups and labour unions to raise and spend unlimited amounts on **independent expenditure** in support of candidates.
- There is no limit (as there is in the UK) on the number of political ads that can be broadcast on television.
- Large numbers of well-funded pressure groups – for example, the NRA and wealthy individuals such as the Koch brothers – spend and donate generously to campaigns and causes that support their aims. Most of this money is raised/spent via Super PACs/PACs (see pp. 99–100).
- There is an enduring belief among candidates and parties that spending more than one's opponents can give the edge in competitive races. Better-funded candidates are more likely to win, though the 2016 presidential race was an exception – Trump spent $398 million versus Clinton's $768 million.
- Some individuals and groups give to a wide range of candidates and to both parties. As a businessman and property developer in the 1990s and 2000s, Trump donated to both Republican and Democrat candidates. 'I give to everybody. When they call, I give… And do you know what? When I need something from them…I call them. They are there for me.'

Independent expenditure Money raised for election campaigns that is not raised or controlled by the candidates themselves. In theory, there must be no co-ordination between these funds, 'soft money', and the 'hard money' raised by the candidates.

Hard money Money raised and donated to official campaigns. TV ads produced by the candidates themselves are accompanied by an endorsement voiceover stating that the candidate approves the ad. Hard money is subject to limits on the size and frequency of donations.

Soft money Money raised and spent independently of the candidates' official campaign, but which supports their candidacy, or more frequently is spent attacking their opponents. It is not subject to limits regarding how much is raised and spent.

Exam practice answers and quick quizzes at **www.hoddereducation.co.uk/myrevisionnotesdownloads**

Should campaign finance be reformed in the USA?

REVISED

There are arguments for and against reforming the financing of campaigns (see Table 8.4).

Table 8.4 Should campaign finance be reformed?

Yes	No
Election expenditure has got out of control in recent years.	In fact, allowing for inflation, 2016 saw slightly less spent than in 2008 and 2012.
The emphasis on fundraising distracts elected representatives from focusing on doing their real job: making laws and listening to all their constituents.	Candidates still need to listen to a wide range of their voters and often call 'town hall' meetings to hear their constituents' views. The reason Congress nowadays is so unproductive is to do with hyper-partisanship and not the distraction of fundraising.
The cost of elections means that only the personally wealthy or well connected, e.g. Trump, can really afford to enter politics and get anywhere. It heightens the elitist nature of US politics.	Fundraising and political donations are a crucial part of the democratic process. They allow supporters to show additional loyalty to their favoured candidates and causes.
The Supreme Court's recent decisions have added to the problem. The issue needs to be tackled by a constitutional amendment that expressly allows Congress to limit campaign finance.	The Supreme Court has merely upheld crucial First Amendment rights regarding freedom in political activity when striking down some campaign reform laws. It also upheld the Bipartisan Campaign Reform Act in 2003 (*McConnell* v *FEC*).
Reforms are desperately needed to plug loopholes like the emergence of Super PACs, 527 and 501 (c) groups. There is too much political influence already from wealthy vested interests, which raises the issue of corruption and 'buying votes' in Congress. See the Trump quote on p. 76.	Whatever reforms are passed, the wealthy will always find loopholes: 'Money, like water, will always find an outlet' – Supreme Court justices Stevens and O'Connor.
Matching funding has all but died out. In 2000, the Federal Election Commission (FEC) paid out nearly $240 million in matching funds. In 2016, it paid out only $1 million as nearly all candidates chose to opt out.	

Direct democracy

There are three main types of direct democracy: ballot initiatives (also known as propositions), recall elections and referendums.
- Ballot initiatives are the most significant/widely used.
- The USA only has direct democracy at state level. This allows no scope for national referendums as in the UK.
- Laws concerning direct democracy vary considerably from state to state. California is often seen as the most high-profile state to make frequent use of ballot initiatives.

Exam tip

It can be a good synoptic point to make that variation in direct democracy between states is an example of federalism in practice.

- It adds to the number and cost of elections, but also enhances opportunities for political participation.
- The system is popular (in 2016, 162 measures in 35 states were voted on) but popularity is decreasing overall – the peak number was 274 (1998).

Referendums

`REVISED`

Referendums are measures/laws drawn up by state legislatures and put to the people to accept or reject. They are a means of vetoing state laws/proposals. They are sometimes known as legislature referred measures.

- Some states require certain measures, e.g. changes to the state constitution or state taxes, to be approved by both the state legislature and a popular vote.
- Some states have a mechanism called a popular referendum where recently passed but controversial state laws can be put to a popular vote which can veto them.
- 2016 example – a measure in Alabama to alter the procedures for the impeachment of state officials.

Initiatives/citizens' propositions

`REVISED`

Unlike referendums, these measures are initiated by voters themselves. States require varying numbers of signatures for a measure to get on the ballot.

- In 2016, 71 initiatives were voted on.
- Although state-based, frequently initiatives in one state are copied/followed in others – for example, nine states in 2016 held votes on legalising marijuana (passed in eight).
- Other recent and common initiatives have included gay marriage and raising the state minimum wage.
- They promote the notion of **legislative laboratories**.

> **Legislative laboratories** The process whereby a law trialled in one state then spreads to others via ballot initiatives. This has been the case recently for legalising certain soft drugs.

Recall elections

`REVISED`

Recall elections are probably the least significant form of direct democracy as they are rarely used and even less frequently successful in removing state-level elected officials.

- They allow state-level officials, such as the governor, to face a public vote before their term has expired.
- A recall election often involves a large number of signatures to be collected, hence they are rarely used. For example, it takes around 790,000 signatures to recall the governor of Michigan. Many recall petitions are also rejected by local courts on various technical grounds.
- The vast majority of recall petitions concern low-level state officials such as local mayors or state senators. Only three governors have ever faced recall elections. The last was Scott Walker of Wisconsin in 2012, who survived. The last governor to lose a recall vote was Gray Davis of California, who lost in 2003 to Arnold Schwarzenegger.
- In June 2018, a local judge in California, Aaron Persky, was successfully recalled for delivering what was seen as an unduly lenient sentence in a sexual assault case. He was the first Californian judge to be recalled for 80 years.

Now test yourself

TESTED ☐

6 Which type of direct democracy is most significant overall?
7 Give an example of an issue voted on in a ballot initiative.
8 Is direct democracy on the increase?
9 Which state is most commonly associated with direct democracy?
10 Who initiates referendums?

Answers on p. 127

Typical mistake

Do not fall into the trap of thinking federal politicians, such as the president, can be recalled. The only way to remove a president mid-term is by impeachment.

Debate over direct democracy: does it help or hinder democracy?

REVISED ☐

There are arguments for and against direct democracy (see Table 8.5).

Table 8.5 **Direct democracy: does it help or hinder democracy?**

Helps	Hinders
Allows voters to have a direct say in framing laws. A 'purer' form of democracy.	Can lead to the 'tyranny of the majority', namely voters passing laws that negatively impact on a minority, e.g. requiring driving tests to be in English only.
	Ordinary voters may not always understand complex laws fully. They may also vote for unsustainable measures, such as cutting state taxes but increasing spending on public services, which can lead to huge budget deficits.
Promotes variation in laws between different types of state, e.g. liberal and conservative.	Can lead to inconsistencies and variation in laws between states.
Improves accountability of state-level officials.	Often simply a political tactic used by 'sore losers', or those unhappy with specific policies. Undermines representative government.
Adds another check and balance to state executives and legislatures between elections.	Adds another opportunity for stalemate and stalling over important issues. Limits ability to govern.
Increases opportunities for political participation.	Adds to democratic overload.
Pressure groups often get involved, e.g. the NRA publicly backed a 2014 measure in Alabama to strengthen Second Amendment rights.	Involvement of wealthy pressure/interest groups gives them disproportionate influence.

Voting behaviour

Many of the factors that affect voting behaviour are common to both the USA and UK, e.g. class/wealth, geography and age.

- In the USA, race and religion are much more significant than in the UK. So too is the personality of candidates – US politics is more candidate centred, especially at primary level.
- Voting behaviour is complex and is best understood as involving factors that make someone more likely to vote a certain way.
- There is a distinction between primacy factors, e.g. voter profile, and recency factors, e.g. October surprises, as will now be explained.

Primacy factors

Primary factors are long-term influences on voting behaviour, e.g. age, race and political alignment (see Table 8.6).

Table 8.6 **Primacy factors**

Category and statement	2016 examples to support the point
Race: Africans-Americans overwhelmingly vote Democrat, along with Hispanics and Asians. White voters support the Republicans but by smaller margins.	88% of African-Americans voted Democrat, as did 66% of Hispanics and 65% of Asian-Americans. 59% of white voters voted for Trump.
Gender: women are more inclined to vote Democrat, while men trend Republican.	54% of women voted for Hillary Clinton. 53% of men plumped for Trump.
Religion: white evangelical Christians ('born-again') strongly back the Republicans. Non-religious voters strongly trend Democrat.	81% of white evangelicals supported Trump. 68% of those without a religious affiliation voted for Clinton.
Wealth: there is less of a difference than might be expected. Richer voters do not overwhelmingly vote Republican, nor do poorer voters strongly trend Democrat.	Both candidates received 47% of the vote from those earning over $100,000 pa. 53% of those earning under $50,000 pa voted Democrat.
Age: young people tend to vote Democrat, while older voters are more likely to support the Republicans.	55% of under 30s voted Democrat. 52% of over 65s voted Republican.
Self-declared political philosophy: most who call themselves liberals vote Democrat and.	81% of conservatives backed Trump. 84% of liberals backed Clinton.
Sexual orientation: most Americans who identify as LGBT vote Democrat.	78% of those who identified as LGBT voted for Clinton, only 14% voted for Trump.
Geography: small-town, suburban and rural areas favour the Republicans. Large urban areas are usually Democrat strongholds.	90% of urban areas were won by Clinton in 2016. 75–90% of suburbs, small towns and rural areas backed Trump.

Recency factors

Recency factors are short-term influences, on voting behaviour, e.g. issues and the electoral campaign (see Table 8.7).

Table 8.7 **Recency factors**

Factor	2016 examples to support the point
Issues and policies: immigration, trade and foreign policy	Trump emphasised restricting immigration ('Build that wall'), a travel ban on many Muslims and also tariffs on foreign imports – protectionism. He also wanted an 'America first' foreign policy. Clinton strongly opposed all these policies. In every election, politicians will tailor policies to appeal to their base but also hopefully to some independent voters too.
Personalities: candidates' background and experience	Clinton emphasised experience (former First Lady, senator and Secretary of State), Trump emphasised his business record and outsider/anti-establishment status in politics: 'drain the swamp'.
October surprises	Trump and the *Hollywood Access* tape, Clinton and her use of a private email server.
Mood of the nation	Strong populist sentiment, many worries about the future and America's place in the world.

TESTED

11 Below are five examples of voter profiles. Which party, Democrat or Republican, are they most likely to vote for?
   (a) An African-American female living in Los Angeles.
   (b) A gun-owning white male living in rural Arkansas.
   (c) A Hispanic male living in the suburbs of Texas who regularly goes to an evangelical church.
   (d) A young, single, white female living in Boston, who is non-religious.
   (e) A gay white male who lives in a small town in the Midwest and owns several firearms.

Answers on p. 127

> **Exam tip**
>
> It is vital in questions about voting behaviour to recall precise statistics for different groups. Although the figures given in Table 8.6 are for 2016, also quote figures from earlier elections to illustrate both changes and consistent patterns in voting behaviour.

Parties and core voting coalitions

REVISED

Political parties in the USA need support from a wide range of groups to win elections. The core voter coalitions for each party can be summarised as:

- Republicans – white evangelicals, older voters, social conservatives, gun owners, those who live in suburbs/small towns and rural areas, those fearful of large-scale immigration and suspicious of big government.
- Democrats – ethnic minorities, younger voters, social liberals, LGBT voters, urban dwellers, blue-collar unionised workers, supporters of causes such as feminism and gun control.

With core voters, candidates and parties need to ensure that:

- their platforms and policies appeal to all sections of their traditional core voters
- key groups turn out and vote – some have ascribed Clinton's 2016 defeat partly to lower turnout among young voters. 'Getting out the vote' remains very important in winning elections.
- Core voter coalitions are kept loyal by policy pledges designed specifically to appeal to them. Hence Republicans usually adopt pro-life positions to appeal to the religious right, while most Democrats advocate some measure of gun control.

> **Typical mistake**
>
> Do not see these categories as mutually exclusive, but rather regard these voter blocs as inter-linked and overlapping. For example, those living in large cities are more likely to be from an ethnic minority, younger and more socially liberal.

Re-aligning elections

Certain elections are seen as key turning points in voting behaviour and are thus known as re-aligning elections. They represent long-term shifts in voting behaviour and political allegiances.

Pre-1980 example: 1968 Nixon versus Humphrey

REVISED

The 1968 election took place against a growing polarisation in US politics.

- Ultra-conservative Republican candidate from 1964, Barry Goldwater, had already energised the right with his book *Conscience of a Conservative* and Ronald Reagan had made a landmark speech, 'A Time for Choosing', the same year. The 'New Right' had also become increasingly concerned with robustly standing up to the USSR in the midst of the Cold War.

- Meanwhile, many Democrats had moved to a more progressive stance on issues such as civil rights earlier in that decade. The peace movement, the hippy culture and more liberal attitudes to abortion and gay rights were also emerging as causes embraced by many on the liberal side of US politics.
- The 1968 election thus took place against a backdrop of growing social and political divides in the USA, which was partly reflected in the positions and platforms of the two parties and candidates.
- Nixon ran as the champion of the 'silent majority', who rejected the radicalism and cultural liberalism of the time. There was a strong focus on law and order and 'traditional values'.
- This was the first example of the Republicans' 'southern strategy', i.e. appealing to disaffected whites in the South alienated by the passage of civil rights legislation.
- It permanently disrupted the Democrats' formidable New Deal coalition established by FDR in the 1930s, as the 'Solid South' abandoned the Democrats. In 1968 the Deep South largely backed third-party segregationist candidate George Wallace. In subsequent elections, white southern conservatives voted Republican.
- The election ushered in an era of Republican dominance in presidential elections, with the party winning seven out of the ten contests between 1968 and 2004.

Post-1980 example: 2016 Trump versus Clinton

The 2016 election was the first example for more than 50 years of victory by a political outsider, someone with no political experience.

- It was viewed as a victory for populism over experience and mainstream politicians. On the Democrat side, outsider candidate Bernie Sanders came quite close to defeating Hillary Clinton in the primaries.
- Many previously loyal Democrat white blue-collar workers in Rust Belt states such as Michigan and Ohio swung behind Trump, attracted by his promises on jobs and trade. It was his (narrow) victories in states such as Wisconsin (last won by a Republican back in 1984) that tipped Trump over the winning line in 2016, despite him losing the popular vote.
- It revealed the growing gap between urban and multi-ethnic America and the largely white exurban/small town/rural America.
- The main shifts in voting behaviour need to be carefully analysed, however. Many voter blocs roughly stayed the same as in 2012. For example, white evangelicals remained loyal to Trump despite his public moral lapses, such as two divorces and several affairs. Equally, African-Americans solidly backed Clinton.
- The main change was among less well-educated whites in Upper Midwest states such as Michigan and Wisconsin and also in Ohio. For example, Ohio whites went for Trump 62–33%, a considerable improvement from 2012 when Romney won 57% of the white vote.
- There is some suggestion that whites in the Upper Midwest/Rust Belt states might be voting more like whites in the South, i.e. Republican. This could be caused in part by the decline of organised labour (trade unions), which traditionally played a key role in getting out the white blue-collar vote for the Democrats.

> **Exam tip**
>
> It would be wise, if using 2016 as an example of a post-1980 re-aligning election, to stress that it is still early days to be confident of a permanent shift in the white blue-collar vote. Some of the trends in 2016 could be down to the personalities of the two candidates.

Split-ticket voting

Split-ticket voting is the ability to vote for candidates from different parties for different elected posts in the same election – for example, in 2016, voting for Trump (Republican) as president but voting for a Democrat as one's House member or senator.

- The growth of **hyper-partisanship** has made this much less common.
- The opposite of split-ticket voting is straight voting.
- In 2016, every state where there was a Senate race voted for the same party's candidate as president. By contrast, in 1988 the figure was only around 50%.
- There were also only 35 (8%) split congressional districts in 2016.
- There remains considerable split ticketing with local state elections. For example, 'blue' Massachusetts elected a Republican governor in 2014, while 'red' Montana elected a Democrat governor in 2016.
- Voters might split their ticket for a number of reasons – personality of the candidates, desire to balance power between the parties or different issues dominating in different levels of elections.

> **Hyper-partisanship**
> Political parties in fierce disagreement with each other and largely voting the same way in Congress. This is a growing feature of US politics since the 1980s.

Abstention

America has traditionally had high levels of voter abstention and low turnouts. In addition, some groups are more likely to vote than others – **differential abstention**.

> **Differential abstention**
> Explaining why turnout is traditionally lower among certain groups, e.g. youth, than others.

Evidence

REVISED

Only 55.7% of the voting age population (VAP) turned out for the presidential race in 2016, though this did represent around 87% of registered voters. By contrast the 2017 UK election saw a turnout of just under 69%.

- Turnout is even lower for primaries, typically under 30%. It was just 5.5% in the Kansas caucuses. It is also lower for the mid-terms: around 36% in 2014.
- Wealthy Americans are much more likely to vote than poorer Americans, though African-American turnout now often surpasses that for whites, as it did for example in 2012: 66.6% of eligible African-American voters compared with 64.1% for white voters. In 2016, though, African-American turnout fell by 7% while the white turnout rose slightly to 65.3%. Latino turnout is considerably lower than for both these groups: 47.6% in 2016.
- Women are more likely to vote than men (63% to 59% respectively in 2016) and older voters are more likely to vote than younger ones. For example, in 2016, 70% of those aged over 70 voted compared with just 43% of 18–24-year-olds.

> **Exam tip**
>
> Be aware how turnout has not fallen consistently. From a low point in 1996, it rose in the subsequent three elections and was slightly higher in 2016 compared with 2012, though lower compared with 2008.

> **Typical mistake**
>
> It is not true that all racial minorities have low turnouts. African-Americans who are registered to vote often vote in high numbers.

Reasons for low voter turnout in the USA

REVISED

There are various reasons for low turnout among voters:
- Multiple elections (democratic overload).
- Lack of voter choice as there are only two main parties.
- Political alienation: some groups, especially poorer and younger voters, may feel politicians do not listen to them and policies either are not delivered or fail to benefit them – there is a lack of **political efficacy**.

> **Political efficacy** The sense that one's vote actually makes a difference and is not wasted.

- Voter registration requirements, i.e. voters in the USA must positively 'opt in' to get on to the voter list. In the UK, the state registers all voters automatically.
- New voter ID laws, e.g. in Texas, that require voters to produce government-issued photo ID such as a passport. This is often seen as discriminating against ethnic minority and poorer voters.
- Many races are not competitive: wasted vote syndrome.
- Gerrymandering in states increases the uncompetitive nature of many House districts, which can be especially relevant to mid-terms turnout.
- Many living in the USA are ineligible to vote, e.g. the large number of ex-felons.
- The negative nature of much political campaigning – 'attack ads'.

Summary

You should now have an understanding of:
- the main features and factors in US election campaigns
- how the Electoral College works and key arguments for and against
- the purpose and nature of primaries and caucuses and their advantages/disadvantages
- the functions of national nominating conventions
- the importance of money in US elections and the debate over campaign finance reform
- how direct democracy works in the USA and the associated pros and cons
- the main influences on voting behaviour
- key statistics concerning voter profiles
- the main voting blocs for each party
- split ticketing and its recent decline
- why relatively few Americans vote.

Exam practice

1 Explain and analyse three ways in which any one US election before 1980 could be defined as significant regarding changes in voting behaviour. [9]
2 Explain and analyse three functions performed by national nominating conventions in the USA today. [9]
3 Analyse, evaluate and compare the arguments in the passage below for and against the Electoral College as a method of selecting the US president. [25]

Despite many criticisms, especially in 2000 and 2016, the Electoral College overall remains the preferable way to choose the US president. Recent mismatches between the popular vote and the actual winner are the rarity, not the norm. True, the margin of victory is sometimes distorted, but this has no practical impact on the power of the newly elected president, unlike the distortions produced by the UK's majoritarian electoral system. The criticism of 'faithless electors' is largely misplaced; their actions have never affected the overall outcome of a presidential election and have even occasionally provided an outlet for protesting about political issues in the states. The Electoral College reinforces the state-based nature of elections and allows states considerable freedom to adapt and modify the indirect system of election in a manner of their choosing. The alternatives to the Electoral College seem superficially attractive but would simply replace one problem with others.

Yet, there are arguments on the other side. One unfair result is one too many: can the USA really call itself a true democracy if the candidate with the most votes fails to win? Any system that puts the likes of George W. Bush and Donald Trump into the White House against the will of the majority also cannot be justified. In summary, despite its flaws and quirks, the alternatives to the current system for selecting the president are as problematic as the institution they would seek to replace.

Source: original material written by the author of this book for educational purposes, 2018

Answers and quick quiz online

ONLINE

9 Political parties

Two parties dominate the USA: the Democrats and the Republicans.

- Traditionally, each party has been broad-based and diverse: 'big tent' or 'catch-all' parties.
- Over the past 20 or so years, the parties have become narrower, more ideological and increasingly distinct from each other. This phenomenon is termed hyper-partisanship.
- US parties are much less centralised than those in the UK. Local state parties remain very important. Primaries also weaken the power of national parties.
- There remain significant divisions and factions within each of the two main parties.

The main divisions between Democrats and Republicans

Ideology and values

REVISED

Both parties share a number of common beliefs:

- A strong attachment to capitalism and the free market.
- Commitment to a republican system of government.
- A preference (for party advantage) for the majoritarian/First Past the Post electoral system. Both would suffer from any change to a more proportional voting system, which would encourage the rise of third parties and independents.
- A belief that America should maintain a powerful presence in the world and remain the pre-eminent global power.

However, they differ in a significant number of areas (see Table 9.1), which translate into specific policy differences (see Table 9.2).

Table 9.1 **Key differences in values between Republicans and Democrats**

Republicans	Democrats
Stronger emphasis on individual freedom/self-help, especially in economics.	While wishing to retain capitalism and wealth differentials, a greater acceptance of government help to aid the poorest.
Belief that religion/faith (especially Christianity) should have a greater public role and presence.	While certainly not anti-religion, a distinct desire to retain a clear separation between church and state.
Clear commitment to upholding the rights of gun owners (Second Amendment).	Strong emphasis on the rights of minorities under the Equal Protection Clause (Fourteenth Amendment).
Traditionally keen on 'small government' and states' rights, though this has diminished somewhat since 2000.	More supportive of a larger and more active federal government (FDR's New Deal, etc.).

> **Exam tip**
>
> It is worth commenting in any response that US parties have traditionally been less ideological than their UK counterparts. While the Republicans nowadays can clearly be labelled conservative, the Democrats might best be termed liberal/progressive, certainly not socialist.

Policy differences

The difference in values/ideology is reflected in their stances on various issues (see Table 9.2). Note though that there are still politicians in both parties who would take a different stance.

Table 9.2 Republicans and Democrats: policy differences

Policy	Republicans	Democrats
Taxes	Keen to keep as low as possible and support cutting the taxes of the wealthy/corporations as a way of generating jobs and stimulating the economy, e.g. 2017 Tax Cuts and Jobs Act reduced corporate tax rate from 37% to 21%.	Less willing to cut taxes for the wealthy and keener to put money in the pockets of ordinary Americans, e.g. in 2010 Obama cut payroll taxes by 2% while reviving an inheritance tax on estates worth over $5 million.
Gun control	Very reluctant to introduce or support tougher gun laws, though willing to consider minor changes such as banning 'bump stocks'. Strong ties to the NRA. Many Republican-controlled states, e.g. Mississippi, back 'open carry'.	More supportive of gun control measures such as tighter background check. President Clinton supported the Assault Weapon Ban passed by Congress in 1994; it expired in 2004 and despite attempts was not renewed.
LGBT rights	Generally hostile to expansion of gay rights and same-sex marriage. Some Republican states have tried to pass 'bathroom bills'. A few moderate Republicans are more sympathetic, e.g. former senator Mark Kirk.	Generally supportive, reflecting a socially liberal approach. President Obama came round to endorsing equal marriage. He signed a bill repealing 'Don't Ask, Don't Tell' in 2010 that had previously banned gay Americans from serving in the military.
Healthcare	Oppose the extension of publicly funded/managed healthcare. Strongly opposed to Obamacare. Since 2016, though, have found it harder to agree on an alternative. Largely see healthcare as an individual responsibility for working people.	Many support a greater provision of state healthcare. Obamacare/Affordable Care Act seen as a major step towards reducing the number of working Americans without health insurance. Many favour the 'public option' for medical insurance.
Immigration	Keen to restrict immigration, especially from Mexico and Latin America. Trump strongly supported a border wall: 'Build that wall.'	Favour immigration reform and particularly making citizenship possible for many existing illegal immigrants such as the 'Dreamers' (those brought to the USA illegally as children).
Abortion	Strongly pro-life and anti-abortion, e.g. George W. Bush signed the Partial-Birth Abortion Ban Act in 2003. Keen to de-fund organisations such as Planned Parenthood. Reflects strong ties with the 'religious right'.	Increasingly pro-choice, though 63 House Democrats did back the 2003 Partial-Birth Abortion Ban Act. Reflects links with feminist/socially progressive movements such as EMILY's List.

Now test yourself

1 Which party is more likely to defend the rights of gun owners?
2 Which party is more likely to support and speak up for the rights of minority groups?
3 If you are strongly in favour of a woman's right to choose regarding abortion, which party are you more likely to support?
4 Which party is keener to cut taxes for the wealthy in order to allow wealth to 'trickle down'?
5 Which party do you suspect is most likely to believe in the reality of climate change and support measures to reduce the use of fossil fuels?

Answers on p. 127

> **Exam tip**
>
> If answering a question to do with party policies, refer to platforms rather than manifestos, which is much more a UK term.

Changes since the 1960s

Both parties have become more polarised for a number of reasons:

- Democrats such as LBJ came out in support of civil rights in the 1960s. This alienated many conservative white Democrats in the South, who were deliberately targeted by the Republicans.
- The Republicans became increasingly conservative, not least under President Reagan (1980–88) and were more and more associated with tax cutting, a 'hawkish' and '**neo-con**' foreign policy (e.g. the invasion of Iraq) and the religious right.
- The impact of the so-called 'culture wars', often seen as a clash between progressive, liberal and metropolitan America and those espousing traditional values.
- Some argued that parties themselves were in decline as institutions by the early 1970s. The subsequent renewal and polarisation of the two parties has firmly laid to rest that belief.
- The growing polarisation is generally agreed to have begun in earnest in the 1980s and to have been accentuated by the clearly political efforts by Republicans to impeach Bill Clinton in the 1990s.
- The presidencies of G.W. Bush, Obama and Trump have only increased this divide. In April 2018 Trump had an approval rating of 89% among Republicans and just 9% among Democrats. By contrast, Republican president Eisenhower in the 1950s enjoyed approval rates of over 60% from Democrats in his first year in office.
- Evidence of polarisation can partly be measured by voting patterns in Congress. For example, not a single Republican senator voted for the Affordable Care Act (Obamacare) in 2010 and not a single Democrat senator voted for Trump's tax cuts bill in 2017.
- Senate nomination votes are also good indicators of partisanship and party polarisation. For example, in 2018 Supreme Court justice nominee Brett Kavanaugh saw all but one Republicans present vote for his confirmation while all but one Democrats voted against his nomination, meaning he was confirmed on a 50–48 vote. By contrast, in 1993, Justice Ruth Bader Ginsburg was confirmed 96–3.

Neo-con Standing for neo-conservative, this approach to foreign policy involved an interventionist and military approach in tackling global terrorism and America's enemies overseas. It is most associated with the presidency of George W. Bush (2000–08) and especially his vice president, Dick Cheney.

Typical mistake

'The Party's Over' thesis was not implying that political parties were on the verge of disappearing or that they had become identical, but rather that they had become too weak organisationally.

Exam tip

Although it is right to stress growing partisanship in Senate confirmation votes, be cautious about making sweeping generalisations. The new director of the CIA, Gina Haspel, was only confirmed by the Senate in May 2018 thanks to six Democrats crossing the floor to support her.

Party decline or party renewal?

REVISED

Table 9.3 considers of whether parties are facing decline or renewal.

Table 9.3 **Party decline or renewal?**

Evidence for party decline	Evidence for party renewal
The growth in split-ticket voting up until the 1980s.	The decline in split-ticket voting in recent years. Record low in 2016. See p. 83 for more details.
Rise of primaries – reduced the control of the 'party machine' in candidate selection.	Democrats have unelected super-delegates comprising 20% of delegates at their national nominating convention.
Party leaders in Congress and even presidents often struggle to persuade legislators to toe the party line.	Growing party unity/partisanship in both congressional votes generally and Senate confirmation votes.
Growth of candidate-centred campaigning; parties are rarely mentioned in ads or literature.	Emergence of much more coherent policy platforms among both parties, e.g. Gingrich and the Republicans' 'Contract with America' in 1994.
The rise of pressure groups as an alternative focus for political participation.	The strong influence of many pressure groups on particular parties, e.g. NRA and the Republicans.

Factions within parties

As 'big tent' parties, Republicans and Democrats still contain supporters with differing views. This is reflected in party factions. Among key ones are:
- Republicans: Freedom Caucus (very conservative, especially fiscally) and the Tuesday Group, an informal group of around 50 more moderate Republican congressmen/women.
- Democrats: Blue Dogs (fiscally conservative) and New Democrats (more centrist and socially liberal).

Party factions are significant for a number of reasons:
- Especially when a party is in power, they can make it much harder for the leadership to get a measure through Congress, as seen for example with 'Trumpcare' in 2018. Factions generally matter less in opposition.
- They reflect the diversity of the USA and 'big tent' parties.
- Factions often highlight the different political traditions of America's regions. Hence most conservative Democrats will come from the South or Midwest, while moderate Republicans (e.g. Susan Collins) are more likely to hail from the North East.
- The fluctuating fortunes of various factions can reflect the overall direction of the party and recent polarisation. For example, Blue Dog numbers have declined significantly in recent years from 54 in 2010 to just 14 in 2017.

Party organisation

US parties are much more decentralised and loosely organised than their UK counterparts. State parties continue to play an important role, reflecting the federal make-up of the USA.
- This has led some to refer to a 100-party rather than a two-party system.
- US parties play little part in candidate selection due to primaries.
- Primaries can see certain candidates being endorsed and publicly supported by leading politicians. This by no means guarantees victory in the primaries though – for example, the Republican Alabama Senate primary in 2017 was won by the controversial Roy Moore, despite most Republican 'establishment' figures such as Mitch McConnell supporting his opponent, Luther Strange.
- There are no official leaders as such; instead there are party leaders in the Senate and House and the president/presidential candidate. Again, perhaps this is an example of the informal separation of powers principle.
- There are chairs of the national bodies (**RNC** and **DNC**) but these posts are not that influential and rarely high profile, e.g. Ronna McDaniel, chair of the RNC in 2018.
- Both parties have so-called 'Hill committees': these are bodies that work for the election of more Republicans/Democrats to the House and Senate, e.g. the NRCC (National Republican Congressional Committee). The committees primarily seek to raise funds for strong candidates in competitive races or those considered vulnerable to defeat by the opposition.

Exam tip

As well as citing 'Contract with America' as a historic example of a more unified party platform, you could reference the Democrats' 'Better Deal' programme, launched in 2017 for the 2018 mid-terms, focusing on 'Better Jobs, Better Wages, Better Future'.

Revision activity

Research the four key Hill committees (NRCC – National Republican Congressional Committee, DCCC – Democratic Congressional Campaign Committee, NRSC – National Republican Senatorial Committee and DSCC – Democratic Senatorial Campaign Committee) and identify their key functions and activities.

RNC Republican National Committee.

DNC Democratic National Committee.

Now test yourself

6 Are the following statements about parties true or false?
   (a) The conservative wing of the Democrats is growing in size and influence.
   (b) There are no national bodies in either party.
   (c) State parties remain very important.
   (d) Primaries weaken the power of the party leadership.
   (e) Obama was the most divisive president to date, in terms of how he was viewed by Democrats and Republicans.

Answers on p. 127

Third parties and independents

As stated above, there are no strong third parties in US politics. In particular, there are no significant regional parties akin to the nationalists, such as the SNP, in the UK.

- Established third parties include the Greens and the Libertarians.
- In the 115th Congress (2017–19) there were no independents/third parties represented in the House. The two independent members of the Senate (Angus King from Maine and Bernie Sanders from Vermont) caucused with the Democrats and frequently voted alongside them too. Bernie Sanders sought the Democrat presidential nomination in 2016.
- The last independent/third-party presidential candidate to receive a significant share of the vote was Ross Perot (19%) in 1992.
- The last independent/third-party candidate to win any Electoral College votes was George Wallace (46 votes) in 1968.
- In 2016, independent and third-party candidates secured around 5% of the vote, up from just 1.7% in 2012.

Why do third parties and independents do poorly in US elections?

Reasons include:
- the majoritarian electoral system
- lack of media coverage – e.g. televised debates where third parties and independents are rarely featured. Last time was Ross Perot in 1992
- the 'big tent' nature of the two main parties
- primary system enables voters to have a wide choice within the main parties and offers opportunities for outsider candidates, e.g. Trump
- cost of US elections (Ross Perot was a billionaire who largely self-funded in 1992)
- often portrayed as extremist and/or inexperienced in public office
- voters' willingness to vote for 'the lesser of two evils'
- often strict **ballot access laws** – Jill Stein (Greens) failed to get on the ballot in three states in 2016.

> **Ballot access laws** Each state has different requirements for candidates/parties to get their names on to the election ballot in the first place. This often involves getting thousands of signatures – one of the harshest is in Oklahoma, which requires a newly qualifying party to submit a petition signed by 5% of the number of votes cast in the previous election.

The significance of third-party and independent candidates

Although lacking presence in elected posts, this is not to say third-party and independent candidates are irrelevant in US politics.

- In close races they can indirectly determine the final outcome of the contest, such as Ralph Nader's performance in Florida in 2000.
- If their policies are seen to be gaining in popularity, these policies are often taken up by the main parties (cooptation) – for example, Ross Perot's promise to bring down the budget deficit and work towards a balanced budget.

Typical mistake

Do not confuse the lack of third-party/independent representation in Congress with the absence of any significance.

Summary

You should now have an understanding of:

- the key values and policies of the two main parties
- the main developments in the parties from the 1960s and reasons for the current polarisation
- the debate over party decline vs party renewal
- factions within each party
- how US parties are organised
- the role and significance of third parties and independents in US politics.

Exam practice

1 Explain and analyse three ways in which the Republican Party has changed in terms of ideology and policies over the past 40 or so years. [9]
2 Explain and analyse three ways in which US political parties could be said to be experiencing renewal rather than decline. [9]
3 Analyse, evaluate and compare the arguments in the passage below for and against the dominance of hyper-partisanship in US parties today. [25]

US political parties have become increasingly polarised and partisan in recent years, especially as a result of the 'culture wars' between a largely white, religious and conservative America and a more multi-racial and secular progressive America. We can thus confidently talk of a Red America and a Blue America; Purple America is largely a myth. The Republican Party stands unequivocally for gun rights and the Second Amendment and is pro-life and anti-abortion. No one arguably personifies this more than Donald Trump, who sharply divides opinion in the USA. Voting records in Congress show this only too clearly. For example, the most recent Supreme Court nominee, Brett Kavanaugh, was confirmed by the Senate very largely along party lines. The same applies to recent Democrat nominees.

Yet before one assumes that party unity is everything, there is an alternative scenario. Members of Congress are still willing to and capable of defying their party leadership. For instance, 12 House Republicans voted against President Trump's $1.5 trillion tax cut bill in December 2017. Both parties have internal coalitions with powerful factions that can pull the party in different directions. The party leadership in Congress has few weapons in its arsenal to persuade rebel legislators to toe the party line. There may not be much of Purple America left, but the parties in Congress are far from being the tightly disciplined machines one might assume.

Source: original material written by the author of this book for educational purposes, 2018

Answers and quick quiz online

10 Comparative politics: electoral and party systems

Elections and electoral systems

Areas of similarity and contrast are shown in Table 10.1.

Table 10.1 Elections and electoral systems: similarities and contrasts

Common features	Distinctive features
Majoritarian (FPTP) electoral system ● Both nations use majoritarian or First Past the Post electoral systems that generally result in two-party dominance and a clear outcome to elections.	● The UK uses other electoral systems as well for non-Westminster elections, such as AMS for devolved assemblies. Recent election results from the UK have not necessarily resulted in strong single-party government, e.g. the 2010–15 coalition government and a minority Conservative government after the 2017 election.
Two-party dominance ● As a result of a majoritarian electoral system, parties in both countries can win power on a disproportionate share of the vote. For example, in 2017 the Conservatives won 42.4% of the overall vote but 48.9% of seats. Likewise, in the 2016 House elections, the Republicans won 49.1% of the vote but 55.4% of seats. In both countries, third parties and independents are considerably disadvantaged by the electoral system.	● Two-party dominance is considerably greater in the USA. The regions in the UK are certainly not a two-party duopoly, with the SNP and Plaid Cymru being significant forces in the devolved assemblies. Even in the Commons, the Liberal Democrats, until 2015 at any rate, were a major presence. By contrast, third parties and independents are almost non-existent in Congress. The USA has no experience of coalition or minority government because the executive branch is directly elected – there can only be one victor in a presidential contest.
Regularity of elections ● Both countries have regular fixed-term elections. The maximum length of a Westminster Parliament is fixed at five years. The 2011 Fixed-Term Parliaments Act was intended to avoid premature parliamentary elections in the UK. ● Elections for Congress are staggered, with only a third of the Senate up for election at any one time. The two-year term of the House often means that control there passes from one party to another in the middle of a presidential term. This creates divided government, which makes it harder for a president to get legislation through Congress.	● In reality, while the regularity of US elections remains fixed, those in the UK remain flexible. For example, Theresa May called an early general election in 2017 and bypassed the Fixed-Term Parliaments Act.
Use of direct democracy ● Both countries make use of direct democracy such as referendums.	● There is no provision for a national referendum or ballot measure in the USA; direct democracy is entirely state based. ● Direct democracy in the UK is used exclusively for major constitutional issues such as EU membership or devolution. It is not used for social issues. Nor can ordinary voters propose legislation as they can in many US states via ballot initiatives.

→

Common features	Distinctive features
Focus of election campaigns ● In both countries, election campaigns are often focused as much on the shortcomings and poor records of opponents as on the positive virtues of one's own campaign – negative campaigning. In the USA, the Trump campaign in 2016 was probably as crude and personal as any election campaign, with Trump describing his opponent as 'crooked Hillary' and encouraging calls to 'lock her up'. Political attacks in the UK tend to be less abrasive, but Theresa May did comment that Jeremy Corbyn would be 'alone and naked in the negotiating chamber' in the Brexit talks during the 2017 election campaign.	● The level of personal attacks is probably harsher and more vitriolic in the USA; in part this is due to 'attack ads' aired on TV, a genre non-existent in the UK. Also, US campaigns, especially at primary level, tend to be more candidate than party focused. UK general elections are more about the competing promises and pledges in party manifestos. TV debates in the UK are also much more recent (2010) than in the USA (1960) and incumbent Prime Minister Theresa May declined to participate in 2017. Such an action would probably be unthinkable in the USA for a president seeking re-election.

Two-party systems in the UK and the USA

Table 10.2 considers the two-party systems in both countries.

Table 10.2 Two-party systems: similarities and contrasts

Similarities between the UK and USA	Differences between the UK and USA
● Both parties contain a range of views and could be described as internal coalitions. These differences are frequently ideological. One can talk within the Labour Party of a hard-left faction such as Momentum and within the Conservative Party of moderate One-Nation Tories. Equally, in the USA there are very conservative Tea Party Republicans alongside more moderate Republicans.	● There are issues that create divides and tensions within the parties on each side of the Atlantic. In the Conservative Party, the main split at the time of writing is Brexit/Remain, while in the USA the main Republican divides are arguably over immigration and trade and just how conservative to be on social issues and gun control.
● Each of the main parties in the USA and the UK can now safely be labelled as conservative or liberal/broadly progressive. They are ideologically distinct. For example, both Conservatives and Republicans generally favour lower taxes, dislike 'big government' and favour tighter immigration policies. By contrast, Labour and the Democrats put greater stress on the rights of minorities as identified by race, sexuality, etc., support 'green' environmental policies and are more willing to accept a degree of wealth distribution from rich to poor via taxation.	● The Conservative Party is more socially progressive than the Republicans on issues such as abortion and same-sex marriage. Also, Conservatives strongly support the NHS while no Republican would favour a 'socialised healthcare system'. By contrast, the Democrat Party is more moderate and centrist than the Labour Party under Corbyn. One can confidently say that nowadays, Republicans sit to the right of the Conservatives and Democrats are more to the right than the present-day Labour Party. ● The British parties have long been more ideologically based and distinct (as implied by terms such as liberal and conservative), while this is a much more recent development in the USA.
● Both parties exhibit internal party rebellions and revolts, e.g. Democrat members of the House who voted against Obamacare and Labour MPs who rebelled over tuition fees.	● Party unity in the legislature remains much lower in the USA compared with the UK.

Similarities	Differences
• The two parties nowadays represent largely contrasting policies and viewing blocs.	• The dominance of the central or national party is much weaker in the USA, in part due to the size and diversity of the country. Primaries also contribute to a weakened sense of central control over state parties.
• Both parties are strongly in favour of retaining the current electoral system for national elections (and in the USA for pretty much every other election), precisely because it greatly aids their dominance in Parliament/Congress.	• In some elections, primarily European and for the devolved assemblies, Labour and Conservatives do compete under alternative electoral systems.

Now test yourself

TESTED ☐

1 Which party, Labour, Conservative, Republican or Democrat, is generally associated with the policies below? NB: Some policies are associated with more than one party.
   (a) Low taxes.
   (b) Greater help for the poorest in society.
   (c) Strong defence of the rights of gun owners.
   (d) Green energy policies and a desire to reduce carbon emissions.
   (e) A universal healthcare system funded and largely run by the state.
   (f) A strong commitment to the rights of minority groups.
   (g) A strong nuclear deterrent.
   (h) Making abortion much harder to access.
   (i) Detaching the country from international agreements and multinational bodies.
   (j) Tough policies on immigration.

Answers on p. 127

Typical mistake

If discussing the ideology and policy positions of the Democrats compared with the British Labour Party, do not use the term 'socialist'. Other than perhaps Bernie Sanders (who technically is an independent), very few on the liberal/progressive side of the Democrat Party would self-identify as socialist. The Democrats have never had a Clause IV!

Third parties and independent candidates in the UK and the USA

Third parties (but less so independents) enjoy much more success, popularity and visible representation in the UK.

• Independents (such as Ross Perot) have been more prominent in the USA than in the UK, perhaps reflecting the wider emphasis on candidates' personality and character and the opportunities for self-funding in elections. Even in the USA, though, they have rarely posed a serious threat to the two main parties.

• For third parties and independents in the USA there is less opportunity for high-level media appearances such as television debates. By contrast, in the UK, party election broadcasts have been made by a range of third parties in recent years, including UKIP and the Greens. They have also been involved in some televised debates.

• Third parties and independents are handicapped by ballot access laws in many states.

• In the USA, the most successful independents have tended either to be very rich personally (e.g. Ross Perot) or to have a strong regional base (e.g. George Wallace in 1968).

• Third parties and independents in the USA historically have often been characterised as extremists ('If you liked Hitler, you'll love Wallace' jibe in 1968). By contrast, the most prominent third party in the UK, the Liberal Democrats, is centrist.

Explaining differences between US and UK party systems

- The UK has a range of electoral systems for elections. Where more proportional systems are used (e.g. European elections), this offers greater opportunities for third parties to secure representation and thus visibility.
- The primary system in the USA allows wider choice within the two dominant parties. Intra-party elections enable another level of voter choice within what are still 'big-tent' parties.
- There is no tradition of strong regional parties in the USA, unlike the nationalist parties of the UK.
- The cost of US elections makes it harder for new parties to emerge and develop in the first place. Few groups or individuals would want to 'invest' in an untried party. Much campaign funding anyhow goes to incumbents, again making it difficult for new parties to get off the ground.

The debate over party finance

In both countries, there is considerable concern over the role of money in election campaigns. Similar worries include:
- Too much money comes from a relatively small number of individuals or interest groups.
- Those who donate are looking for favours and rewards in return.
- This in turn leads to fears over buying influence and 'politicians for hire'. Democracy, it is argued, is being sacrificed on the altar of campaign donations.
- There is debate over how far, if at all, the state should fund parties and political activity.
- Both countries share a desire (among most) for political donations to be public and transparent.

There are, however, additional concerns in the USA:
- The escalating cost of elections (well in excess of $6 billion in 2016), as compared to the much more tightly regulated world of UK elections where the combined Conservative/Labour/Liberal Democrat spend in 2017 was around £36 million.
- The undermining of campaign finance reforms by Supreme Court judgements such as in the Citizens United and Speechnow cases (2010) – this makes comprehensive reform all the more difficult and unlikely. This stems from interpretations of the First Amendment: is the freedom to raise and spend vast amounts of money for political and campaign purposes a protected right alongside freedom of speech?
- The decline and virtual extinction of matching funding.

> **Exam tip**
>
> If comparing attitudes and rules concerning election spending, bring in the First Amendment as a useful synoptic link from the constitution topic. The UK has no equivalent entrenched right that can be interpreted by the courts.

Main differences between the USA and the UK in campaign finance

REVISED

Campaign finance differs in the following ways:
- Campaign finance rules are much slacker in the USA than in the UK. Measures such as the Bipartisan Campaign Reform Act have been seriously weakened both by court judgements (see p. 94) and by wealthy donors/interest groups finding loopholes, e.g. 527 and 501 (c) groups. Its UK counterpart, the Political Parties, Elections and

Referendums Act (PPERA), by contrast, has not been challenged on anything like the same scale.

- Campaign spending by both parties and candidates is more tightly regulated in the UK. This applies equally to referendums. For example, in the EU referendum, the leading campaign group on each side was limited to £7 million.
- Pressure groups spend large amounts in US elections via PACs and Super PACs. Such activity is again much more regulated in the UK.

Theoretical approaches to electoral and party systems

Table 10.3 outlines the theoretical approaches to electoral and party systems.

Table 10.3 **Electoral and party systems: theoretical approaches**

	Aspects to analyse
Structural The role of political institutions	• How parties in the USA are much more decentralised and weaker than in the UK. • The greater range of views within the two main American political parties. • The role of the US Supreme Court in shaping rules around campaign finance and how the First Amendment is seen to extend protected rights to pressure groups and corporations. Campaign finance laws in the UK, by contrast, are decided solely by Parliament.
Rational The role of individuals	• The different types of voting system used in the UK and the USA and how this affects voting behaviour and impacts on third parties and independents. • How the opportunity for ballot initiatives in the USA makes this a method and campaign focus for many pressure groups. • How and why many individuals or groups which want to influence policies and elections in the USA will donate to or create PACs/Super PACs.
Cultural The role of shared ideas and culture	• The stronger tradition of third parties in the UK, e.g. Liberals/Liberal Democrats. • The longstanding involvement of US pressure groups in political campaigning and political funding. • The much bigger scale of expenditure on elections and campaigns in the USA, not least due to laxer laws about political advertising on television.

Summary

You should now have an understanding of:
- similarities and differences between the electoral systems of the UK and the USA
- how the parties in each country differ in terms of organisation/unity and also policies
- why the USA remains a two-party dominant system, while the UK has strong elements of a multi-party system

- why third parties do better in the UK
- how election campaigns differ, especially in terms of political advertising on television and the role of pressure groups
- the debates and issues over political funding in both nations.

Exam practice

1 Explain and analyse three ways in which rational theory could be used to study direct democracy in the UK and the USA. [9]
2 'Third parties are doomed to failure in the USA but not in the UK.' Analyse and evaluate this statement. [25]
3 'There is huge common ground in terms of policy between the Democrats and the UK Labour Party.' Analyse and evaluate this statement. [25]

Answers and quick quiz online

ONLINE

11 Pressure groups

Political pluralism in the USA

Pressure groups are many and varied in the USA and reflect the country's political pluralism.

- This is best understood as the representation of and participation by numerous and competing groups organised around class, racial, ethnic and cultural interests. A huge and diverse nation like the USA will contain many such interest groups.
- The range and importance of pressure groups also result from the First Amendment and guaranteed freedom of political expression.
- Unlike political parties, pressure groups do not seek elected office or fight elections directly but seek to influence policy-makers and voters.
- Many pressure groups face strong opposition from countervailing groups, those that seek a different policy outcome – for example, NARAL Pro-Choice America competes with the pro-life Susan B. Anthony List in lobbying and seeking to influence the abortion debate.
- Critics argue that in reality, there is not a level playing field when it comes to influencing law-makers and that certain groups are much more likely than others to wield influence – **elitist theory**.

> **Elitist theory** The argument that rather than competing equally, some pressure groups, especially those that are well funded and have close ties to politicians and the government, are more powerful than others. This is a key argument in criticising the view that pressure groups enhance democracy.

Types of pressure group

Pressure groups are divided into outsider and insider groups.

- Outsider groups tend to be smaller, less well funded and less well connected. Their aims are often anti-establishment in nature, seeking radical change. Many use direct action such as marches, sit-ins or even violence to gain publicity. A recent example is Black Lives Matter.
- Insider groups are usually well funded, with strong ties to the political establishment, often including links with both main parties. They are much more likely to use lower-profile methods to achieve their aims, such as hiring professional lobbyists to put their case to politicians and federal agencies. Many raise considerable sums via political action committees to spend on election campaigns to support or oppose selected candidates. Some raise and spend money for candidates of just one party; others, such as the pro-Israel group NORPAC, split money more equally between candidates of both main parties.

Pressure groups are also divided into cause and sectional groups.

- Cause (promotional) groups are more altruistic in their aims; they are seeking policy outcomes that will not personally benefit supporters but are (from their perspective) morally right. Groups campaigning for animal rights (e.g. PETA) or the environment (League of Conservation Voters) fall into this category.
- Sectional (or interest) groups seek to defend the interests of their members. For example, the AARP (American Association of Retired Persons), with 37 million members, seeks to uphold the rights of retired/older Americans. Labour unions such as the AFL-CIO also fall into this category, as do employers' organisations.

Exam practice answers and quick quizzes at **www.hoddereducation.co.uk/myrevisionnotesdownloads**

- Some groups are best described as hybrid. Thus the NRA both seeks to defend the cause of the right of Americans to bear arms (Second Amendment) and represents the interests of gun owners.

Now test yourself

TESTED

1 Are the following pressure groups cause/promotional groups or sectional/interest groups?
   (a) Service Employees International Union.
   (b) National Association of Realtors (estate agents).
   (c) Everytown for Gun Safety.
   (d) Christian Coalition of America.
   (e) American Civil Liberties Union.

Answers on p. 127

Pressure group tactics and methods

Candidate endorsement and political campaigning

REVISED

Plenty of US pressure groups (unlike their UK counterparts) focus especially on securing the election of candidates favourable to their policy positions and objectives.

- Many therefore make campaign donations via their PACs and Super PACs (the role of PACs is discussed more fully on pp. 99–100). For example, **EMILY's List** raised and donated over $90 million for the 2016 election cycle.
- They often directly endorse candidates, e.g. the American Federation of Teachers publicly backed Hillary Clinton for president.
- Some issue 'score cards' at election time to their members showing candidates' voting records, e.g. the NRA in 2016 awarded an A grade to Ted Cruz (Texas) and an F grade to Tammy Baldwin (Wisconsin).

> **EMILY's List** A pressure group that works for the selection and election of progressive pro-choice women to Congress. All the money distributed via the group goes to liberal, female Democrat candidates. EMILY stands for Early Money Is Like Yeast.

> **Typical mistake**
>
> It is not actually true that pressure groups donate large sums directly to candidates as such campaign contributions (hard money) are capped by law. Most spend money independently of candidates' official campaigns.

> **Exam tip**
>
> Be aware that some pressure groups also work for the defeat of candidates whom they feel have a very poor record, e.g. League of Conservation Voters' 'dirty dozen' list.

Lobbying Congress, state legislatures and federal agencies

REVISED

US pressure groups are able to lobby various **access points** in the USA. These include not just Congress but also federal agencies and state governments. In short, pressure groups follow the scent of power wherever it is found.

- This is probably the most effective method employed by pressure groups, if often low profile.
- Many large pressure groups have offices in Washington DC and state capitals ready to supply specialist policy information to legislators and bureaucrats.

> **Access points** The different levels and institutions of government and decision making that pressure groups will target and lobby to gain influence.

- Some pressure groups use professional lobbying firms such as Squire Patton Boggs – 'K Street'.
- Many lobbyists are former members of Congress or former high-ranking federal bureaucrats. This is a controversial practice known as the **revolving door syndrome**.
- Lobbying federal agencies such as the Environmental Protection Agency (EPA) can be especially effective. Much of the detailed regulation is drawn up by such agencies after Congress passes a law. For example, after the 2010 Dodd–Frank Act (passed to tighten up banking regulations after the financial crisis), by 2014 federal agencies had written only 200 of the 400 required regulations. The delay was due to extensive lobbying by the banks themselves. Representatives from Goldman Sachs and JP Morgan met with relevant federal agencies more than 350 times between 2010 and 2012.

> **Revolving door syndrome**
> When former legislators or bureaucrats go from positions in the legislature or executive to lucrative jobs as lobbyists, e.g. in 2016 former senator David Vitter from Louisiana went to work for the lobbying firm Mercury after retiring from the Senate.

Lobbying the Supreme Court

REVISED

- Pressure groups of all types draw up and present *amicus curiae* **briefs** for relevant Supreme Court cases. These documents are produced by lawyers and contain detailed evidence and research to try to influence the justices.
- For example, in 2018 a number of Christian groups such as the Christian Coalition of America and some Muslim groups such as the Islamic Society of North America worked together to produce an *amicus curiae* brief against legalising large-scale sports betting.
- The use of *amicus curiae* has grown considerably in recent years. The 2015 *Obergefell* v *Hodges* case (same-sex marriage) saw a record 148 such briefs presented to the Court. By contrast, only 6 briefs were submitted for *Brown* v *Board of Education of Topeka* and 23 for *Roe* v *Wade*.
- Pressure groups often also lobby the Senate during the nominations process for the Supreme Court. For example, many women's and civil rights groups strongly lobbied against Robert Bork's nomination in 1987. Similarly, in 2018 many liberal groups, including 88 civil rights organisations, lobbied against Kavanaugh's nomination.

> *Amicus curiae* **brief** Latin term meaning 'friend of the court' brief. A written argument submitted to a court of law by a person or group that has an interest in the case being considered. Pressure groups often try to use *amicus curiae* briefs to influence the court and employ expert lawyers to write them.

Direct action

REVISED

Direct action is most commonly used by new and/or outsider groups to gain publicity and media attention.

- It often takes the form of mass demonstrations but can include strikes or sit-ins.
- It was a major tactic of the civil rights movement in the 1950s and 1960s and of Martin Luther King, who led the March on Washington in 1963.
- Some direct action can result in riots and can become associated with violence – for example, five police officers were ambushed and killed at a Black Lives Matter protest in Dallas in July 2016.
- Following the school shooting in Parkland, Florida, in February 2018, hundreds of thousands of school students took part in 'March for Our Lives' to campaign for tighter gun control laws. There were also school walkouts.
- Direct action is generally regarded as less effective than lobbying in the long term as publicity is hard to sustain and can often be linked to disorder/lawbreaking.

> **Typical mistake**
> Just because direct action often makes the news headlines, do not assume it is automatically more powerful. Scenes of violence can often alienate voters and policy-makers. Low-key methods such as lobbying are usually more effective.

Boycotts are used in various ways:
- Some civil rights campaigners use them – for example, Rosa Parks and the Montgomery bus boycott in 1955–56.
- Increasing economic pressure is used by businesses and even celebrities to put pressure on law-makers.
- After the Parkland shootings, Wal-Mart raised the minimum age for purchasing firearms and ammunition to 21.
- Bruce Springsteen cancelled a concert in North Carolina in 2016 in protest at the state passing a 'bathroom bill'.

> **Exam tip**
>
> In any answers about methods and tactics, mention that pressure group targets are not always federal government or Congress but often state governments and governors.

Factors affecting success

Success factors include:
- resources: money and size of membership
- status: insider or outsider
- strength of groups with opposing objectives
- political climate: which party controls Congress/occupies the White House
- public mood – for example, support for gun control increases markedly after school shootings, though interestingly, so too do donations to the pro-gun lobby
- links with legislators and bureaucrats
- ability to organise at a grassroots level and to organise large-scale events such as marches
- endorsement and support from politicians and celebrities, e.g. Lady Gaga supporting the #MeToo movement.

Election funding

Many pressure groups are heavily involved in election campaigns, especially in raising and distributing money to favoured candidates.
- Most pressure group donations follow predictable party patterns, with labour unions and pro-choice groups overwhelmingly backing Democrat candidates – for example, in 2016 the labour sector donated more than $29 million to Hillary Clinton's campaign. By contrast, over 86% of donations from the agribusiness sector went to Republican candidates.
- A disproportionate amount of pressure group funding goes to incumbents. Many less ideological groups prefer above all to back winners. Pressure groups could thus be said to reinforce the **incumbent advantage** and that of Washington insiders.
- Being supported or indeed targeted by a major pressure group does not guarantee election night victory. Only 3 out of the 12 candidates on the LCV's 2016 'dirty dozen' list were defeated.
- PACs and Super PACs are the principal legal means by which pressure groups raise and donate funds for election campaigns.
- A PAC is a political committee that raises and spends 'hard' money contributions for the specific purpose of electing or defeating candidates. There are legal limits on how much PACs can receive and donate to candidates and parties. They can give up to $5,000 to a candidate per election cycle and up to $15,000 annually to a national political party. PACs may also receive up to $5,000 each from individuals, other PACs and party committees per year. Donations and donors must be formally recorded and made public, and the PAC must be formally registered with the Federal Election Commission.

> **Incumbent advantage**
> The benefits enjoyed by existing senators and House representatives, such as better funding and greater name recognition.

- Many pressure groups have a PAC. For example, the NRA's PAC is the Political Victory Fund, which spent over $30 million in the 2016 presidential race.

Super PACS

REVISED

Super PACs emerged after the 2010 Citizens United/Speechnow cases, which essentially granted First Amendment rights of political expression to corporations, labour groups and pressure groups.
- It means they can effectively raise and spend unlimited amounts on election campaigning, provided the expenditure is independent and uncoordinated with candidates' official campaigns and political parties. In essence, Super PACs raise and spend 'soft' money.
- Their growth has significantly increased the amount of political donations. Most leading candidates have Super PACs supporting their campaigns, e.g. Hillary Clinton's main Super PAC was Priorities USA Action.

Do PACs and Super PACs play too big a role in US elections?

REVISED

Table 11.1 considers this question.

Table 11.1 **Is the role of PACs and Super PACs in US elections too great?**

Yes	No
PACs and Super PACs are increasingly significant in fundraising for elections and are a vital method of getting round campaign finance limits.	Rich candidates (Trump) can partly self-fund anyhow and matching federal funds are available for candidates who self-limit overall campaign expenditure. Also, blame recent Supreme Court decisions for the growth of Super PACs.
The vast amounts raised and spent by PACs/Super PACs favour well-connected and 'establishment' candidates.	Superior funding does not guarantee victory. Clinton outspent Trump in 2016 and lost.
Rich donors wield too much power and influence over elections, leading to charges of legalised bribery.	The right to make political donations large or small is a fundamental political right in a democracy.
Legislators are too much in the pockets of powerful and wealthy pressure groups and individuals.	Members of Congress cannot be 'bought' and can never forget the views of voters as well as donors.
PACs and Super PACs undermine the role of political parties.	Party allegiance remains strong and party labels essential for successful candidates. Most pressure groups align with their 'natural' party anyhow, e.g. LGBT groups such as the Human Rights Campaign normally support and endorse Democrats.

Pressure groups and iron triangles

Pressure groups are a vital part of the tight policy networks often termed 'iron triangles'.
- The term was first coined by President Eisenhower, who in 1961 referred to the dangers of the 'military–industrial complex', namely the strong and costly ties between the defence industry, Washington politicians and bureaucrats.

- This is especially true of corporate groups. For example, major pharmaceutical companies often have close ties with the Food and Drug Administration (part of the federal bureaucracy), while also donating to legislators who sit on relevant congressional committees, such as the House Subcommittee on Agriculture, Rural Development, Food and Drug Administration, and Related Agencies.
- Iron triangles are seen as working against the public interest and instead favouring powerful corporate interests.

> **Exam tip**
>
> If evaluating the overall significance of iron triangles, provide a specific example, not just the general principle.

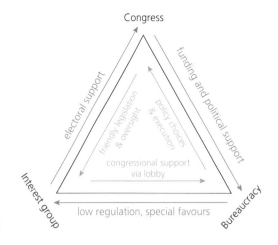

Figure 11.1 Iron triangle

Source: Wikimedia Commons

TESTED ☐

Now test yourself

2 What are the three 'sides' of an iron triangle?
3 What must a Super PAC *not* do?
4 Which court cases allowed the formation of Super PACs?
5 Which movement in modern America first used economic boycotting effectively?
6 Which constitutional amendment rights do pressure groups reflect?

Answers on p. 127

Are US pressure groups too powerful?

Table 11.2 addresses this question.

Table 11.2 **Are US pressure groups too powerful?**

Yes	No
Potential of corruption and undue influence as many lobbyists are former congress(wo)men or bureaucrats – revolving doors.	Lobbyists are regulated to an extent, e.g. 2007 Honest Leadership and Open Government Act.
Legislators are afraid of upsetting key pressure groups, e.g. many Republicans and the NRA.	Represent and reflect the vast array of groups, beliefs and causes in an increasingly diverse USA.
Advice from pressure groups is one-sided and can harm the wider public interest – iron triangles.	Provide legislators and bureaucrats with useful technical information and advice when it comes to drawing up bills and regulations.
Undermine and weaken political parties.	Political parties in the USA are already weak and 'big tent'. Many pressure groups simply 'pitch up' under a suitable 'tent' anyhow, thus consolidating and shaping the internal coalitions that constitute US parties.
Not all groups and interests are equally powerful and well organised, e.g. drug companies vs patient groups.	Enable participation outside elections and enhance the fundamental freedoms of speech and association (First Amendment).
Can lead to accusations of influence being bought by the best-funded groups and legislation being partly written by corporate groups.	Can increase levels of scrutiny of both Congress and the executive.

Summary

You should now have an understanding of:
- how pressure groups in the USA fit into its political pluralism
- the main categories of pressure groups
- the methods and tactics commonly employed by pressure groups
- the role of pressure groups in election funding and the part played by PACs and Super PACs
- whether or not US pressure groups are too powerful.

Exam practice

1 Explain and analyse three methods used by US pressure groups.   [9]
2 Explain and analyse three reasons why iron triangles are seen as powerful in US politics.   [9]
3 Analyse, evaluate and compare the arguments in the passage below for and against the view that pressure groups have too much power in US politics.   [25]

> Pressure groups can be seen as a vital aspect of US democracy. They enable a diversity of views, not least those of minorities, to be voiced and heard. They also ensure that legislators at both state and national level are kept abreast of voters' views. With much legislation being extremely complex and technical, many members of Congress and indeed federal bureaucrats are only too happy to have expert and knowledgeable input from pressure groups and their lobbyists. Although the advice may be one-sided, in a pluralist political environment such as that of the USA, there will always be a range of advice on offer; their power over legislation is thus ultimately beneficial to good governance. Most policy areas have a wide range of interest groups which seek to be heard. For example, when it comes to minorities, there is the well-established NAACP (National Association for the Advancement of Colored People), but also the less prominent Organization of Chinese Americans and various Hispanic groups. Hence, no one group has a monopoly on influence.

> It is true, though, that some would argue that pressure groups in the USA have too much power, not least over political parties. For example, the NRA has a near stranglehold over the Republicans. Also, the 'revolving door' syndrome encourages corruption as former senators frequently take on lucrative jobs with K Street lobbyists when they retire or lose an election. There is much to be said for the view that pressure groups rarely, if ever, benefit the national interest and instead are only interested in the selfish interests of their members or cause. In summary, pressure groups in the USA have more power than they can handle responsibly.

Source: original material written by the author of this book for educational purposes, 2018

Answers and quick quiz online

ONLINE

12 Comparative politics: pressure groups

Areas of similarity

In both countries, pressure groups have the same fundamental aims, namely to influence legislation, regulations and government policy making.

- The same typology can be applied to pressure groups in both the USA and the UK, such as insider/outsider groups and cause/sectional groups.
- Many of the tactics are similar, such as insider groups using lobbying and outsider groups relying more upon direct action.
- Both the USA and the UK have seen a growth in membership and influence in pressure groups in recent years. The National Trust, for example, had 5 million members in 2017, while the AARP had over 37 million. In both cases, though, much of this membership may be due to the material benefits of belonging, such as free entry to historic sites or discounted insurance – **chequebook membership**.
- In each country, pressure groups provide an opportunity for political participation and representation of a wide range of groups and viewpoints, and reflect the wider pluralist nature of liberal democracies.
- Despite the pluralist theory, in reality some groups in each country are seen as considerably more powerful and influential than others. Groups backed by big business and corporate interests, for example, are normally more powerful than consumer groups, which are less well funded and well organised.
- The 'revolving door' is active in both countries, with many former legislators and senior civil servants/federal agency workers going on to lucrative posts with lobbying companies after leaving government or elected office.

> **Chequebook membership**
> Those who join a pressure group primarily for the benefits provided. Such members may be far less interested or active in the political and lobbying campaigns of groups.

Areas of difference

Table 12.1 looks at the areas in which pressure groups differ between the two countries.

Table 12.1 **Pressure groups: areas of difference**

	USA	UK
Access points	Far more due to: • federalism (state governments have many primary legislative powers) • role and importance of the Supreme Court – *amicus curiae* briefs • checks and balances/separation and sharing of powers, e.g. equal legislative powers of Senate and House • sheer number of elections, including primaries and direct democracy.	Fewer due to: • more unitary system of government despite recent trends towards devolution • power remaining centralised in the hands of the Westminster government • Brexit – should mean less focus on lobbying EU institutions such as the European Commission in Brussels • UK courts having fewer powers to influence policy direction and legislation. For example, they cannot strike down laws as unconstitutional.

→

	USA	UK
Involvement in election campaigns	Very considerable because: ● First Amendment rights and recent Supreme Court cases have allowed pressure groups (and others) to spend virtually unlimited amounts in election campaigns, though most of this will be 'soft money' expenditure ● key roles played by PACs and Super PACs ● laxer laws about TV advertising mean well-financed pressure groups such as the NRA run ads supporting, or more usually attacking, election candidates.	Much less important because: ● there are tight laws on election and campaign expenditure, e.g. the pro-Brexit group, Vote Leave, was investigated by the Electoral Commission for exceeding the £7 million spending limit by diverting £625,000 via a pro-Brexit youth group – BeLeave ● there are no direct equivalents of PACs and Super PACs ● there are strict laws on political advertising on terrestrial television channels ● by law, many charities are not allowed to make political donations and trade unions need approval from members to set up political funds.
Lobbying	● Far more organised and commercialised. There is no UK equivalent of K Street. ● Target a wide range of institutions, including the courts, state governments as well as Congress and federal agencies. ● Targeting individual legislators is more likely to yield results as party ties are weaker. Lobbying members of Congress via their voters can be especially effective.	● Still focuses very much on central government (see above under 'Access points'), not the regions. ● Lobbying Parliament and individual MPs is less likely to be successful due to stronger party unity. ● Trade unions have historically played a larger role, especially when there have been Labour governments – 'beer and sandwiches at No 10'. This declined under Blair, but the current Labour leadership has strong ties to certain key unions, e.g. Unite.

Are pressure groups more successful in the USA or the UK?

USA

The USA features:
● heavy involvement in election campaigns and associated expenditure
● many groups that are extremely well funded and highly organised, with strong links to policy-makers
● a large number of access points due to both the separation of powers and federalism
● lobbying and importance of the Supreme Court; landmark decisions have a major bearing on public policy
● the influence of K Street lobbyists
● weaker political parties and federal agencies with power to draw up important regulations
● strong ties between certain pressure groups and the main parties. Few Republican politicians can afford to alienate the NRA; few Democrats can oppose the positions of Planned Parenthood on abortion.

UK

In the UK:
● there are strong ties between Labour and the trade unions, which represent their main financial backers

- equally, the Conservatives traditionally enjoy the backing of many in the business community
- the existence of national/regional referendums provides important and additional foci for pressure group involvement.

Theoretical approaches to pressure groups

Table 12.2 looks at the various approaches.

Table 12.2 Theoretical approaches to pressure groups

	Aspects to analyse
Structural The role of political institutions	• Access points and how they vary in number and importance. • The importance in the USA of the Supreme Court as a focus for lobbying. • The lobbying (at least until Brexit) of EU bodies where many important regulations are drawn up.
Rational The role of individuals	• The attraction in both countries for lobbying firms in recruiting former legislators and bureaucrats who 'know the system'. • The focus in the USA on targeting individual legislators who are more likely to change their vote in Congress, compared with British MPs. • The preference in both countries for discrete lobbying over direct action as the strategy for gaining positive policy outcomes.
Cultural The role of shared ideas and culture	• The historic link in the UK between the Labour Party and the trade union movement. • The tradition in America of individual political expression (First Amendment rights). • The importance of direct action in both countries for more marginalised and minority-orientated groups to gain publicity, e.g. the civil rights movement.

Now test yourself

TESTED

1 Which country has a more international dimension to pressure group lobbying?
2 How can a US pressure group seek to influence the Supreme Court?
3 In which country do trade unions wield the most influence?
4 Are corporate interests more powerful in the USA or the UK?
5 Which country has far looser rules about spending by pressure groups at election time?

Answers on p. 127

Summary

You should now have an understanding of:
- the key differences and similarities between pressure groups in the UK and USA
- the relative power and influence of pressure groups in both countries

- how to apply the three theoretical approaches when comparing UK and US pressure groups.

Exam practice

1 Explain and analyse three ways in which rational theory could be used to study the influence of pressure groups in the UK and in the USA. [9]
2 'Pressure groups are far more powerful and prominent in the USA compared with the UK.' Analyse and evaluate this statement. [25]
3 'The main difference in tactics between US and UK pressure groups is their involvement in the judicial branch of government.' Analyse and evaluate this statement. 25]

Answers and quick quiz online

ONLINE

13 Civil rights

Civil rights and civil liberties are protected by the US Constitution and may be modified by Supreme Court rulings.

- Pressure groups such as the NRA and the NAACP play an important role in campaigning for rights.
- One of the most important struggles for civil rights has been the campaign for racial equality in the USA.

Protection of civil rights and liberties

Civil rights and civil liberties are protected in the USA in the ways outlined in Table 13.1.

Table 13.1 **Protection of civil rights and liberties in the USA**

Method	Protection
The Constitution	<ul><li>The framers of the Constitution wrote the document with the aim of protecting citizens from an overly powerful government.</li><li>A codified system of checks and balances was designed to limit the powers of each branch of government.</li><li>The US Supreme Court was established in Article III of the Constitution, giving citizens a court of final appeal if they feel that their rights have been infringed.</li><li>By designing an entrenched Constitution, with a complex amendment process, the framers aimed to prevent the rights set out within it from being easily removed by future governments or legislatures.</li><li>See Chapter 1, pp. 14–15, for details of how effectively the Constitution protects civil rights.</li></ul>
The Bill of Rights	<ul><li>The ten amendments in the **Bill of Rights** were intended to protect the civil liberties of US citizens from the actions of government.</li><li>Examples include:<ul><li>the First Amendment (freedom of religion, speech, press and assembly)</li><li>the Second Amendment (the right to keep and bear arms)</li><li>the Sixth Amendment (the right to a fair trial)</li><li>the Eighth Amendment (which prohibits cruel and unusual punishments).</li></ul></li></ul>
Subsequent amendments to the Constitution	<ul><li>When it was first ratified (1791), the Bill of Rights applied only to free persons, not slaves, and women were not treated equally. Further amendments to the Constitution were required to ensure that the rights of *all* Americans were protected:<ul><li>The Thirteenth Amendment (1865) abolished slavery.</li><li>The Fourteenth Amendment (1868) gave former slaves full citizenship. It contains two important clauses: one giving all citizens 'equal protection' under the law and one stating that a citizen's life or freedoms cannot be removed by the government without 'due process'.</li><li>The Nineteenth Amendment (1920) gave women the right to vote.</li><li>The Twenty-Fourth Amendment (1964) gave Americans the right to vote without needing to pay a tax, thus ensuring that African-Americans (who tended to be poorer) had the same voting rights as whites.</li></ul></li></ul>

Method	Protection
Landmark rulings of the Supreme Court	• The **Supreme Court** has the role of interpreting the Constitution (see p. 55) to ensure that it applies to civil rights and liberties in a modern context. • The Court has made **landmark rulings** that have fundamentally changed the civil rights of Americans. • In *Brown* v *Board of Education of Topeka* (1954), the Court struck down the doctrine of 'separate but equal' that had underpinned segregation in America's South, giving African-Americans the right to share white facilities (see p. 59). This was an important victory for the **civil rights movements**. • In *Roe* v *Wade* (1973), the Court ruled that women had the right to an abortion in the early stages of pregnancy (see p. 60). • In *Obergefell* v *Hodges* (2015), the Court ruled that same-sex couples had the right to marry (see p. 59). • See pp. 55–56 for details of how the Court has interpreted the Bill of Rights to protect citizens' rights.

Bill of Rights The first ten amendments to the Constitution, intended to protect the civil rights and liberties of Americans.

Supreme Court The highest court in the federal judiciary. The Supreme Court is responsible for interpreting the Constitution and only hears cases of constitutional importance.

Landmark rulings Legal rulings that are highly significant because they establish a new legal principle or precedent, or an important change in the interpretation of the existing law.

Civil rights movement The historic campaign for equal rights for African-Americans. It originated in the late nineteenth century but was at its height in the 1950s and 1960s, during which time a series of new federal laws was passed to ban discrimination.

Exam tip

Remember that Congress can give citizens additional rights by passing legislation, e.g. the 1964 Civil Rights Act. However, these laws are not amendments to the Constitution, so are not entrenched and protected.

Typical mistake

Civil rights and civil liberties are often used interchangeably but are in fact different. Civil liberties are the freedoms enjoyed by all Americans, e.g. the right to freedom of speech. Civil rights are additional protections introduced by the government to ensure that groups of citizens are not discriminated against – for example, the 1965 Voting Rights Act outlawed discrimination that stopped African-Americans voting.

Revision activity

One of the best ways to retain information in your long-term memory is to talk to someone else about it shortly after you've learned it. First, make notes from Table 13.1 on how civil rights and liberties are protected in the USA. Then put away your notes and, from memory, try teaching a friend, parent or sibling about the topic. Go back to your notes to fill in any gaps at the end.

Now test yourself

TESTED

1 In which document are civil liberties and rights entrenched?
2 Which amendment gives Americans the right of freedom of speech and religion?
3 What important protection does the Fourteenth Amendment give US citizens?
4 Which landmark Supreme Court ruling gave women abortion rights?
5 Which landmark Supreme court ruling gave same-sex couples the right to marry?

Answers on pp. 127–28

The role of pressure groups in promoting and supporting rights

The right of citizens to form pressure groups is itself an important civil liberty, part of the rights of free speech and assembly defined in the First Amendment.

- Pressure groups have led many campaigns to support rights: liberal groups have tended to work for the rights of African-Americans, women and the LGBT community, while conservative groups have campaigned for religious rights, the rights of the unborn child and gun rights.
- Groups raise funds and pay for campaigns to influence the public, politicians and the judiciary.
- Public campaigning includes internet-based campaigns, social media, organising rallies and marches, and television advertising.
- Political campaigning involves lobbying Congress, state legislatures and federal and state governments, and making donations to electoral candidates.
- Legal campaigning involves sponsoring legal cases or writing *amicus curiae* briefs (see p. 98).
- Pressure groups play a key role in promoting and supporting rights, although in recent years social movements such as the Black Lives Matter campaign (which campaigns for racial equality), the Women's March (which campaigns for civil rights for women) and #MeToo (which campaigns for an end to sexual harassment and assault) have received considerable public and media attention.

Exam tip

For a question about civil rights and pressure groups, be sure to use specific examples. Learn the examples in Table 13.1 and then, every time you make a point about the role played by pressure groups, you can support it with an example. This will really impress the examiner and will help to ensure that your judgements are substantiated by evidence.

Examples of key pressure groups that promote and support rights in the USA

Table 13.2 gives examples of key pressure groups that promote and support rights in the USA.

Table 13.2 **Key pressure group examples**

Key pressure group examples	Role in promoting and supporting rights
National Association for the Advancement of Colored People (NAACP)	<ul><li>The USA's oldest civil rights pressure group, with more than half a million members.</li><li>The NAACP achieved major successes in the 1950s and 1960s as part of the civil rights movement.</li><li>The NAACP focused on winning civil rights by conventional means, whereas Martin Luther King and other leaders of the civil rights movement employed direct action.</li><li>Funded the landmark Supreme Court case *Brown* v *Board of Education of Topeka* (1954).</li><li>Helped to plan the March on Washington (1963), which included the historic 'I have a dream' speech by Martin Luther King.</li><li>Provided legal representation and aid for civil rights protesters who were arrested by the government.</li><li>Lobbied Congress to pass the Civil Rights Acts of 1957, 1964 and 1968 and the Voting Rights Act of 1965.</li><li>Ran successful voter registration campaigns in the twentieth and twenty-first centuries, to increase the number of African-American voters.</li><li>Currently focused on ensuring that African-Americans receive equal economic, education, health, criminal justice and voting rights.</li></ul>
National Organization for Women (NOW)	<ul><li>Has campaigned for women's rights since 1966.</li><li>Uses mass marches, rallies, peaceful civil disobedience, legal action and lobbying, and supports electoral candidates.</li><li>Unsuccessful in its bid to get the **Equal Rights Amendment (ERA)** ratified.</li><li>Since 2017, new women's social movements such as #MeToo (which offered millions of women an online platform to share their stories of sexual harassment and assault), #TimesUp (which includes a legal defence fund for victims of sexual harassment and assault) and the Women's March have gained more publicity than established pressure groups like NOW.</li></ul>
Planned Parenthood NARAL Pro-Choice America	<ul><li>Planned Parenthood provides abortion services and is a political advocate for access to abortion.</li><li>NARAL works for access to abortion by funding legal action, lobbying politicians and making political donations.</li><li>**Pro-choice groups** argue that access to abortion is a fundamental reproductive right that women are entitled to.</li><li>Pro-choice campaigners have been successful in resisting attempts by **pro-life groups** to overturn *Roe* v *Wade* (1973), but over the past two decades an increasing number of restrictions have been placed on abortions in the USA (see pp. 60–61).</li></ul>
National Rifle Association (NRA)	<ul><li>Considered to be one of the most influential lobbying groups in US politics.</li><li>Has around 5 million grassroots members.</li><li>Its income was more than $330 million in 2015.</li><li>Credited with having exceptional influence within the Republican Party: in 2018 only six Republican members of Congress had not received funding from the NRA.</li><li>More than half of members of Congress in 2018 have received funds from the NRA at some point in their political careers (including 24 Democrats).</li><li>The size of the NRA's financial resources means that it can spend far more than gun-control groups on political donations – the NRA and other gun rights groups have donated nearly $13 million to the congressional campaigns of current members of Congress, whereas lawmakers have received only a total of $570,000 from gun-control groups.</li><li>The same is true for lobbying: in 2017 the NRA and other gun-rights groups spent five times as much as gun-control groups on political lobbying.</li></ul>

→

Key pressure group examples	Role in promoting and supporting rights
	• The NRA's influence in Congress allowed it to resist attempts by politicians such as President Obama to introduce gun control legislation following mass shooting tragedies like the 2012 Sandy Hook Elementary School shooting, in which 20 children aged six or seven were killed. • A majority of Americans support tighter restrictions on the purchase of firearms (67% in 2018) and the grassroots 'March for Our Lives' campaign for gun control (inspired by the mass shooting at a school in Parkland in 2018) has demonstrated the strength of public feeling on this issue. However, the power of the NRA makes it very difficult for gun-control advocates to achieve any meaningful progress.
The Human Rights Campaign	• Lobbies federal and state legislatures to support LGBTQ (lesbian, gay, bisexual, transgender and queer) bills. • Provides funding to support and oppose political candidates, depending on their stance on LGBTQ issues. • However, the main success of the LGBTQ campaign, the legalisation of same-sex marriage in 2015, came about as a result of a Supreme Court decision rather than a political consensus (see p. 59).
US Conference of Catholic Bishops Family Research Group	• Defended civil rights and liberties for religious groups, freedom of religion. • Mostly advocate socially conservative policies, including opposing abortion and same-sex marriage. • Argue for the rights of the unborn child in their anti-abortion campaigns. • Religious groups collectively spend around $350 million per year lobbying Congress. • Number of religious groups lobbying Congress has increased five times since 1970, from fewer than 40 to more than 200 in 2011.
American Civil Liberties Union (ACLU)	• Has over 1.75 million members and a staff of 200 lawyers who defend civil liberties in the courts. • Defends the civil liberties of *all* Americans, including the rights of American Nazis or the Ku Klux Klan, arguing that liberties must be protected for *every* individual (even those with views that many people find abhorrent) or there will be nothing to stop the government from taking away civil liberties entirely. • Has had numerous successes, including the ending of segregation in *Brown v Board of Education of Topeka* (1954) (the ACLU supported the NAACP in its campaign against segregation) and the legalisation of abortion in *Roe v Wade* (1973). • In the twenty-first century the ACLU has won court rulings protecting the right to privacy of lesbians and gay men and against the teaching of intelligent design in science lessons in schools. • Mounted multiple legal challenges to the national security measures introduced after 9/11. However, the Bush, Obama and Trump administrations continued the imprisonment without trial of suspects at Guantanamo Bay and expanded the use of drones and targeted killing overseas. • Campaigns for the rights of immigrants within the USA and also challenged President Trump's 2017 ban on immigration from Muslim-majority countries (resulting in a temporary block on the ban, until it was ruled constitutional by the Supreme Court).

Equal Rights Amendment (ERA) A proposed amendment to the Constitution that would have made it illegal to discriminate on the grounds of sex. It was passed by Congress in 1972 but was not ratified by the necessary three-quarters of state legislatures in time for the 1982 deadline set by Congress.

Pro-choice groups Pressure groups that support a woman's 'right to choose' whether she has an abortion or not, or how she manages her reproductive health. Planned Parenthood, NARAL Pro-Choice America and NOW are all pro-choice groups. Democrats and liberals are generally pro-choice.

Pro-life groups Pressure groups that support the 'right to life' of the unborn foetus or embryo and are therefore anti-abortion. Examples include the Pro-Life Action League and the National Right to Life. Pro-life groups are often supported by Republicans and conservatives and in particular by religious organisations.

Revision activity

Make a set of flash cards for the different pressure groups mentioned in this chapter. Each one should include the group's aims, methods and strengths and weaknesses. Give each pressure group an overall rating out of five for how effectively it has protected rights in America.

Typical mistake

Students might assume that because the Equal Rights Amendment was not passed, US women's rights are unprotected. In fact, their civil liberties still have the same protection as those of male Americans within the Constitution, e.g. the Bill of Rights and other subsequent amendments. The ERA was a missed opportunity to entrench equal rights for women, but Congress has passed laws to prevent sex discrimination, though those laws are not entrenched.

Now test yourself

TESTED

6 What is the name of the biggest gun rights pressure group in the USA?
7 What term is used to describe pressure groups that support abortion rights for women?
8 What term is used to describe a legal brief written by a 'friend of the court', such as a pressure group, in an attempt to influence the outcome of a case?
9 Which high-profile pressure group defends the civil liberties of all Americans, particularly through legal challenges?
10 Which proposed women's rights amendment to the Constitution was not ratified?

Answers on p. 128

Case study: the impact of civil rights on US politics – race

Given the USA's history of slavery, segregation and endemic racism, it is not surprising that its politics have been heavily influenced by race and civil rights. The main aspects are outlined below.

The civil rights movement

REVISED

The movement demonstrated the power of pressure groups, campaigners and religious groups to produce meaningful political change.
● Direct action was used to gain support for the cause.
● The brutality of police and many white citizens was exposed by the widespread use of violence against civil rights campaigners.

- The murder of African-Americans, such as 14-year-old Emmett Till in 1955, demonstrated the dangers faced by black Americans and the profound failings of the criminal justice system to convict those responsible for killings or lynchings.
- The landmark Supreme Court decision in *Brown* v *Board of Education of Topeka* (1954) abolished segregation in the American South.
- Congress passed the Civil Rights Acts of 1957, 1964 and 1968 and the Voting Rights Act of 1965.
- The Twenty-Fourth Amendment (1964) protected African-Americans from discrimination in voting.
- Martin Luther King's 'I have a dream' speech articulated a vision of a world in which people would be judged 'not by the colour of their skin but by the content of their character'. King's inspirational leadership helped to develop new attitudes to race and also modelled African-American leadership, which would ultimately lead to the election of Barack Obama in 2008 as the first black president of the USA.

Affirmative action

REVISED

In an attempt to reverse the inequalities faced by African-Americans, Democrats in the 1960s argued for the use of **affirmative action**.

- Liberals thought this was fair as it took account of the economic and social disadvantages faced by many minorities.
- Conservatives argued that affirmative action is a form of reverse discrimination – by giving African-Americans enhanced opportunities simply because of their race, the right of members of the majority group (whites) not to be discriminated against is infringed.
- This has been a polarising issue in US politics – most Republicans are highly critical of affirmative action (including President G.W. Bush), most Democrats (including President Obama) support it. In 2018 President Trump's administration signalled that it would be investigating and challenging certain affirmative action cases.
- In *Fisher* v *University of Texas* (2016), the Supreme Court ruled that affirmative action was legal, provided that certain criteria were met.

> **Affirmative action** Positive discrimination by employers or universities, or federal or state governments, to favour racial minorities.

Voting rights

REVISED

The 1965 Voting Rights Act made it much easier for African-Americans to vote by removing the restrictions on voting in most states in the American South.

- Turnout among African-Americans grew dramatically, particularly in states where they faced extreme discrimination – for example, in Mississippi turnout increased from 7% in 1964 to 67% in 1969.
- African-Americans became an important group of voters. Politicians began to tailor their policies to attract African-American support and African-American candidates were elected to office.
- However, in *Shelby County* v *Holder* (2013), the Supreme Court ruled that states could impose restrictions on voting, arguing that the country had changed since 1965.
- More than 20 states have introduced voter restrictions, including stricter voter identification requirements. Hispanic and African-American turnout has fallen in states with strict voter identification laws, while white turnout has hardly been affected.

- African-Americans and Hispanics are most likely to vote Democrat, so voter identification laws have the net effect of making it easier for Republicans to be elected.
- Not surprisingly, voter identification laws are generally supported by Republicans and opposed by Democrats.

Incarceration rates

REVISED

Modern civil rights campaigners point to the differing incarceration (imprisonment) rates for African-Americans and whites as evidence that the criminal justice system is failing to provide equal rights.

- In 2016, African-Americans made up 12% of the adult population in the USA but 33% of the prison population. Whites made up 64% of adults and 30% of prisoners.
- The incarceration rate for African-Americans is more than five times that of whites.
- This has an important impact on voting: felony disenfranchisement meant that in 2016 one in every 13 African-Americans of voting age was no longer eligible to vote because of a previous criminal conviction.
- The problem is growing – by 2016 felony disenfranchisement had removed the right to vote from more than 10% of African-Americans in eight states (in 1980 only two states reached this level) and from more than 20% in four states.

Typical mistake

Students might assume that the dramatic differences between African-American and white incarceration is simply caused by a higher rate of crime committed by African-Americans. The evidence does suggest that African-Americans are statistically more likely to commit crimes than white Americans, perhaps because they are also more likely to be socio-economically disadvantaged. However, this does not fully explain the difference in incarceration rates. Although African-Americans and whites both use drugs at a similar rate, African-Americans are six times more likely to be incarcerated for drug offences. This suggests that the law is not being applied equally to both racial groups.

Black Lives Matter

REVISED

The movement began in 2013 when the use of the hashtag #BlackLivesMatter began trending on Twitter after George Zimmerman was acquitted for shooting dead unarmed teenager Trayvon Martin.

- President Obama spoke movingly about Martin's death and expressed his frustration at the racial bias within US society.
- Subsequent police shootings of unarmed African-Americans resulted in street protests and riots, such as the Ferguson unrest in 2014.
- Numerous smart phone videos were posted online showing police brutality towards unarmed African-Americans.
- Campaigners linked to the Black Lives Matter campaign addressed the Democratic National Convention during the 2016 presidential campaign.

Typical mistake

Black Lives Matter is a social movement rather than a pressure group. It began as a hashtag on Twitter and has evolved into a national network of campaigners, with its own website. However, it lacks the centralised organisation or hierarchy of a pressure group.

The rise of the Alt-right

The rise of the **Alt-right** poses a new threat to civil rights.

- President Trump's association with some leading Alt-right figures has led to fears that the gains of the civil rights movement may be at risk from his administration.
- Trump failed to clearly condemn the far right after a liberal protester was deliberately run over and killed at a 'Unite the Right' rally in Charlottesville in 2017, claiming that there was violence 'on many sides'.
- Far-right extremists killed more than 40 people between 2014 and 2016.

> **Alt-right** A political movement made up of individuals who hold a range of far-right beliefs, including white supremacists. It includes neo-Nazis and neo-Confederates (people who believe that the US states that supported slavery in the US Civil War were right).

Revision activity

You are more likely to remember material if you use images as well as text. Find an image online to represent each of the six sub-headings in this section (the civil rights movement, affirmative action, voting rights, incarceration rates, Black Lives Matter and the rise of the Alt-right). Add each image to a PowerPoint slide so that you have six slides. Add text to each slide to cover the main information for each area.

> **Exam tip**
>
> When writing about race in US politics, try to avoid making unsubstantiated assertions, such as claiming that President Trump is a racist. Instead, give specific examples of his actions (e.g. his support of the Alt-right and his failure to condemn the far right after Charlottesville) which will support any conclusions you may reach.

Now test yourself

11 Which Supreme Court decision ended the policy of segregation in the USA?

12 What was the name of the movement for racial equality in the USA, led by Martin Luther King, among others?

13 What is the term for the system of positive discrimination towards minorities used by some employers, higher education institutes or governments?

14 How many times greater is the incarceration rate of African-Americans than of whites?

15 Whose unprovoked violence towards African-Americans has been particularly highlighted by Black Lives Matter?

Answers on p. 128

Summary

You should now have an understanding of:
- the ways in which civil rights and civil liberties are protected by the Constitution, particularly the Bill of Rights and subsequent amendments and by landmark Supreme Court rulings
- the role of pressure groups in supporting and promoting rights through the use of legal challenges, political campaigning, rallies and demonstrations, and the internet and social media

- the impact of the struggle for racial equality on US politics, including the successes of desegregation, the Civil Rights Acts and improved voting rights; the controversy generated by affirmative action; continuing struggles faced by African-Americans as highlighted by the Black Lives Matter campaign; and the rise of the Alt-right.

Exam practice

1 Explain and analyse three ways in which a civil rights campaign has had an impact on US politics. [9]

2 Explain and analyse three ways in which pressure groups play a role in promoting and supporting rights in the USA. [9]

3 Analyse, evaluate and compare the arguments in the passage below for and against the view that citizens' rights are well protected by the US Constitution. [25]

Not for nothing is the USA known as the 'land of liberty': the civil liberties of its citizens lie at the heart of its Constitution, particularly within the Bill of Rights and subsequent amendments such as the Fourteenth, which gives all citizens the right of 'equal protection' and 'due process' under the law. These rights are well protected by the complex process of constitutional amendment and the US Supreme Court has shown repeatedly its determination to protect rights through its interpretation of the Constitution. Most Americans identify strongly with the notion of the USA as a free country and value their rights to free speech, association, religion and press.

Nevertheless, it would be wrong to suggest that citizens have not faced challenges in obtaining their rights. Until 1954 the doctrine of 'separate but equal' allowed legal segregation to prosper in the American South, along with a range of voting restrictions that effectively disenfranchised large sections of the African-American population until the 1960s. *Brown* v *Board of Education of Topeka* was just one of a series of landmark Supreme Court rulings that delivered rights to abortion and same-sex marriage which were far from the intentions of the original framers of the Constitution. These decisions were not authorised by the legislature or the states, but rather depended solely on the judgement of nine justices: a poor basis for determining citizens' rights in a modern democratic society. Nor has the Constitution been able to prevent the increase in government surveillance and control that was the result of post-9/11 national security concerns.

Source: original material written by the author of this book for educational purposes, 2018

Answers and quick quiz online

ONLINE

14 Comparative civil rights

Both the USA and the UK have constitutions that are based on the rule of law and the protection of civil liberties.

- The nature of the US Constitution means that the rights of its citizens are entrenched, whereas those of UK citizens are not.
- Both countries have had debates about the civil rights of women and minorities, but in the USA the rights of gun owners and those with religious beliefs also have a more central role in public discussion of rights.
- The US Supreme Court has played a more important role in the development of civil rights than the much younger, less powerful UK equivalent.

Protection of civil rights

Table 14.1 lists the similarities and differences regarding the protection of rights in the UK and the USA.

Table 14.1 **Protection of rights in the UK and the USA**

Similarities	Differences
• Both the US and the UK legislatures can pass legislation to protect citizens' rights, e.g. the **2010 Equality Act** (UK) and the 1965 Civil Rights Act (USA). • Both the USA and the UK have parts of their constitutions that clearly express the rights of their citizens: the US Bill of Rights and the UK Human Rights Act (1998). • The USA and the UK both benefit from the rule of law and independent judiciaries which are able to make rulings against the government on behalf of individual citizens.	• In the USA, civil liberties are entrenched in the Constitution (particularly in the Bill of Rights and some of the subsequent amendments to the Constitution). This means that they can be removed only by amending the Constitution, which was deliberately made difficult to do in order to protect citizens' rights. • In the UK, civil liberties are not entrenched. The Human Rights Act could easily be removed from the Constitution by a simple Act of Parliament. • In the UK, EU law also protects citizens' rights, although this will cease when Britain leaves the EU. • The US Supreme Court can strike down legislation that infringes citizens' constitutional rights. The UK Supreme Court can only make a declaration of incompatibility with the Human Rights Act, referring the matter back to the government for its consideration. • The ability of the US Supreme Court to make civil rights rulings that effectively act as amendments to the Constitution (as the Court is interpreting the original document in such a way as to produce a change in the law) is not shared by the UK Supreme Court, whose judgements are easily overridden by Parliament.

Equality Act (2010) A law passed by Parliament to bring together many different pieces of equality legislation. This included the Equal Pay Act (1970), the Sex Discrimination Act (1975), the Race Relations Act (1976), the Disability Discrimination Act (1995) and the Employment Equality Regulations (2003 and 2006).

Now test yourself

TESTED

1 Which supreme court has the power to strike down legislation that it considers unconstitutional?
2 Which supreme court's interpretation of the Constitution carries nearly the same weight as a formal amendment to the Constitution?
3 Which document protects UK citizens' rights?

Answers on p. 128

Debates about civil rights issues

Both the USA and the UK have had sustained debates about civil rights. These debates have proceeded along similar lines for some issues, but for others there are significant differences between the two countries.

Balancing civil liberties with the government's duty to protect its citizens

REVISED

This debate arose in response to government action taken to protect citizens from terrorist threats after 9/11.
● The USA PATRIOT Act (2001) increased police and government powers to carry out searches of homes, businesses, telephones and email without a court order.
● In the UK, the Prevention of Terrorism Act (2005) introduced government control orders on terrorist suspects. (This Act was repealed in 2011 and control orders were replaced by a new system of terrorism prevention and investigation measures.)

The rights of LGBTQ people   REVISED ☐

Same-sex marriage was legalised by the UK Parliament in the Marriage (Same Sex Couples) Act (2013), though at the time of writing it remains illegal in Northern Ireland. In the USA it was legalised by the Supreme Court decision *Obergefell* v *Hodges* (2015).

- Both countries have seen legal battles over whether businesses have the right to refuse their services to LGBTQ people. In 2013 the UK Supreme Court ruled that the owners of a bed-and-breakfast broke the law when they turned away a gay couple and in 2018 the US Supreme Court ruled in favour of a Christian baker who refused to make a wedding cake for a same-sex couple. In 2018 the UK Supreme Court upheld the right of a bakery to refuse to make a cake with a slogan supporting gay marriage.
- The rights of trans people are currently being debated in both countries.

Women's rights   REVISED ☐

Both countries had women's suffrage movements which led to some women being given the vote by the UK Parliament in the Representation of the People Act (1918) and all American women receiving the right to vote in the Nineteenth Amendment (1920).

- Subsequent debates have focused on abortion rights, equality and anti-discrimination.
- Most recently the #MeToo and #TimesUp campaigns have focused on sexual harassment and assault.

The USA has taken fewer measures to promote women's equality than the UK.

- The Equal Rights Amendment was not passed and there is no right to paid maternity leave in the USA. However, sex discrimination by employers is prohibited by the Equal Pay Act (1963).
- In the UK women have the right to paid maternity leave and the Sex Discrimination Act (1975) explicitly forbids sex discrimination.
- The UK also has an independent public body, the Equality and Human Rights Commission, which guards against all types of discrimination, including sex discrimination.
- In the UK government, the Government Equalities Office works to develop gender equality policy.

Abortion   REVISED ☐

In the USA, since *Roe* v *Wade* (1973) the debate about abortion rights has been one of the most important political issues. In the UK, abortion has been legal since the Abortion Act (1967).

- Individual MPs may have religious objections to abortion and ministers may even have discussed reducing the length of pregnancies that can be terminated, but the main political parties do not want to remove a woman's right to have an abortion.
- In contrast, abortion divides most Republicans (who are pro-life) from most Democrats (who are pro-choice).
- The US debate is particularly fierce because of America's highly religious society. Around 56% of Americans consider themselves religious, compared with just 30% in the UK.
- Northern Ireland is the only part of the UK where abortion is not legal and will probably be the subject of much future debate after the Republic of Ireland legalised abortion in its 2018 referendum.

The rights of immigrants

REVISED

In the USA debate has focused on the question of what to do with the estimated 11 million illegal immigrants living in the country, particularly those who were brought to the country as children.

- The Trump administration's policy of separating children of illegal immigrants from their parents led to a public outcry and in June 2018 it was discontinued.
- In the UK there has been debate over whether immigrants should have equal rights to use the National Health Service and council housing, and whether deporting immigrants who commit a crime constitutes a breach of their human rights under the Human Rights Act (1998).

The rights of ethnic minorities

REVISED

Both countries have had long-term debates about the extent to which ethnic minority citizens enjoy equal rights to the white majority.

- Black citizens in both countries face a range of inequalities and prejudices, as do many ethnic minority citizens who are Muslims.
- There have been debates in both countries about how far ethnic minorities face discrimination from the police and other government sources and how far they are represented proportionally in different professions, business and the public sector.

Race

REVISED

Debates over civil rights and race are important in the UK, but far less central to politics than in the USA.

- This is because of the USA's history of slavery, which was abolished only in 1865 after a bloody civil war (whereas slavery was abolished within the British Empire in 1834), and the unique system of segregation and racial discrimination that followed it.
- Segregation and discrimination in the USA were challenged by the high-profile civil rights movement in the 1950s and 1960s. There was no equivalent iconic campaign in the UK as there was no policy of segregation to resist.
- The legacy of racial discrimination in the USA has led to lasting socio-economic differences between whites and African-Americans and controversial affirmative action policies which do not exist in the UK.
- In the USA, the Black Lives Matter campaign has highlighted the unprovoked violence faced by African-Americans from the police and

other citizens, as have the National Football League (NFL) players who chose to kneel rather than stand when the national anthem was played before matches.

- The Black Lives Matter campaign has been active in the UK but has not received the same level of publicity as the number of killings by police is so much smaller than in the USA.
- The confrontational attitude of President Trump towards Mexicans and protesting NFL players and his support for the alt-right only served to escalate racial tensions.

Gun rights

REVISED

In the USA gun rights are a major political issue, whereas gun control is almost universally accepted in the UK.

Exam tip

If you're asked to explain the reasons for the differing debates on civil rights in the USA and the UK, be sure to focus on the importance of religion in the USA and its impact on the abortion debate, the role of the Second Amendment in preventing gun-control reforms in the USA and the different histories of race relations. The UK did not have legal segregation or restricted voting rights – as occurred in the USA from the late nineteenth century until the 1950s and 1960s – although the British Empire was underpinned by racism.

Revision activity

Read the information about civil rights debates and make a note of key legislation/judgements/events. Then put away your notes and summarise the topic by speaking for a minute without interruption. You could record your efforts if you have a smart phone and then play back the recording and listen for any obvious gaps in your account. Have another go until you have outlined all the different areas discussed here.

Now test yourself

TESTED

4 Which new law increased government powers of surveillance in the USA after the 9/11 terrorist attacks?
5 Which UK law introduced control orders for terrorist suspects?
6 On which women's rights issue do debates within the USA and the UK differ most?
7 Which country's legislature was responsible for legalising same-sex marriage?

Answers on p. 128

Comparisons of methods, influence and effectiveness of civil rights campaigns

Table 14.2 compares the methods, influence and effectiveness of civil rights campaigns in the USA and the UK.

Table 14.2 Civil rights campaigns compared

Civil rights campaigns	Similarities between the USA and the UK	Differences between the USA and the UK
Methods	• Pressure groups in both countries campaign for civil rights using many similar methods, including marches, rallies, lobbying politicians, direct action and civil disobedience. • Although US pressure groups use the courts more than UK pressure groups do, the rise of judicial review in the UK has led to more pressure groups challenging the government in the courts. • Religious groups in both countries have argued that anti-discrimination legislation can infringe on their right to practise their religion, e.g. the Christian Institute supported the right of a Christian-run bakery in Northern Ireland not to bake a cake with a pro-gay marriage message on it, and the UK Supreme Court ruled in their favour in 2018. In the USA, numerous companies objected to the requirement in the Affordable Care Act (2010) that they should provide healthcare insurance for employees that includes contraception, to which they had religious objections.	• In the UK, there are strict limits on political spending during elections, whereas in the USA there are limits on political donations to individual candidates from individuals or pressure groups, but no limits on their overall political expenditure. • This means that US pressure groups (e.g. the NRA) spend far more on supporting and opposing political candidates than UK pressure groups do (although some UK pressure groups are also important political contributors, e.g. trade unions). • US pressure groups are more focused on influencing the Supreme Court than UK pressure groups are because the US Supreme Court has the power to strike down legislation if it finds it unconstitutional or to make interpretative amendments to the Constitution. US pressure groups therefore fund many legal challenges or submit *amicus curiae* briefs to existing cases.
Influence	• Campaigners for civil rights have changed public attitudes in both countries – open displays of racism, homophobia and misogyny are generally considered unacceptable in modern society.	• In the USA, the rise of the Alt-right suggests that the influence of civil rights campaigns has been limited in some sections of the population, as does the willingness of the American public to vote for President Trump despite his having made misogynistic and racist comments. • Religious campaigns have had more influence in the USA, e.g. the pro-life campaign keeps abortion high on the political agenda. • The NRA has a degree of influence over US politicians that is unparalleled by any civil rights group in the UK.

→

Civil rights campaigns	Similarities between the USA and the UK	Differences between the USA and the UK
Effectiveness	• Pro-choice abortion campaigners have been successful in keeping abortion legal in both countries (with the exception of Northern Ireland). • The UK pressure group Liberty and the US pressure group the ACLU have both been effective in highlighting anti-liberal measures taken by the government, particularly in relation to national security. However, neither group has been able to prevent its government from pursuing controversial methods of dealing with terrorist suspects. • LGBTQ campaigns have seen significant progress in both countries.	• Campaigners for women's rights have been more successful in the UK than in the USA, where women have fewer employment rights than in the UK and their right to have an abortion is constantly threatened. • In the USA the protection of the Second Amendment and the efforts of the NRA have ensured that Americans retain their right to bear arms despite public pressure for gun control and frequent mass shootings. In contrast, UK citizens do not have a right to bear arms, so the Snowdrop Campaign (which followed the 1996 Dunblane Massacre of 16 primary school children and their teacher) was able to achieve comprehensive gun control in 1997. • Both countries still have significant progress to make in terms of ensuring full racial equality, but the Black Lives Matter campaign and the rise of the Alt-right have shown that this is particularly the case in the USA.

Exam tip

When comparing civil rights campaigns, two key differences to emphasise are the greater use of political donations by US pressure groups (the NRA is an excellent example to use) and the greater tendency of US pressure groups to campaign using the courts, in the hope of convincing the Supreme Court to make a landmark ruling in their favour. Many of the greatest successes of US civil rights campaigns have been as a result of landmark rulings by the Court.

Typical mistake

Students may not realise that protecting the civil rights of one group can mean infringing the rights of another group. The 'right to life' movement is effectively a campaign for the civil rights of the unborn foetus or embryo. This brings it into direct conflict with the civil right of women to have an abortion.

Revision activity

Divide a page vertically in two and put a heading on each side: 'Features of US civil rights campaigns' and 'Features of UK civil rights campaigns'. Use the information in Table 14.2 to make two lists of features.

Now test yourself

TESTED ☐

8 In which country do pressure groups use the courts most?
9 In which country do pressure groups spend most on political donations?
10 What argument do religious groups in both countries make to justify their opposition to civil rights legislation?

Answers on p. 128

Theoretical approaches to civil rights

The approaches to civil rights are summarised in Table 14.3.

Table 14.3 Theoretical approaches to civil rights

	Aspects to analyse
Structural The role of political institutions	• The impact of an entrenched US Constitution: the entrenchment of civil liberties in the Bill of Rights and subsequent amendments means that liberties are more protected than in the UK's flexible constitution. • The relative importance of the US Supreme Court: the fact that it can interpret the Constitution to produce a change in the law that has the same effect as a formal amendment to the Constitution means that its judgements have had more impact on the history of civil rights (e.g. *Brown* v *Board of Education of Topeka* (1954)) than the UK equivalent. • The sovereignty of Parliament in the UK: Parliament ultimately decides what civil rights UK citizens enjoy, whereas in the USA the Supreme Court plays a more important role. Civil rights campaigns in the USA therefore tend to invest more in using judicial review to achieve civil rights. • Different rules regarding political donations and spending have resulted in pressure groups spending more on political campaigning in the USA and arguably having more influence over elected representatives.
Rational The role of individuals	• Role of President G.W. Bush and Prime Minister Tony Blair in infringing civil liberties after the 9/11 terrorist attacks, through the use of extraordinary rendition, waterboarding and searches without a court order in the USA and the use of control orders in the UK. • Role of individual leaders in campaigning for civil rights and keeping their cause on the political agenda, e.g. the civil rights movement in the USA benefited from the inspirational leadership of Martin Luther King in the 1960s, whereas post-war UK civil rights campaigns have lacked a figure of the same political stature. • Individuals play a key role in civil rights campaigns in both countries: many campaigns centre on an infringement of an individual's rights and their determination to change the situation (e.g. *Roe* v *Wade* (1973), the Snowdrop Campaign).
Cultural The role of shared ideas and culture	• Respect for the rule of law underpins the effective protection of rights in both countries. • Both countries have a culture that values individual liberty and this is reflected in their constitutions (US Bill of Rights, UK Human Rights Act). • Culture of pluralism allows involvement of pressure groups to protect rights. • Culture of judicial activism and 'legislating from the bench' in the USA: judicial activism can protect rights that were not considered by the original framers of the Constitution, e.g. *Brown* v *Board of Education of Topeka* (1954), *Roe* v *Wade* (1973) (though some conservatives would argue that *Roe* v *Wade* ignores the rights of the unborn child). • Following the 9/11 terrorist attacks, a new culture of fear and protectiveness led to governments in both countries taking measures that have been criticised for reducing individual rights. The fact that President Obama continued many of President G.W. Bush's national security measures might suggest that this culture, generated by difficult circumstances, was more important than the role of individual leaders. • Religious groups are much more dominant in US culture, which helps to explain why religious rights play a more prominent role in civil rights debates in the USA than in the UK.

11 Which important principle is respected in both countries and is essential for the protection of civil rights and liberties?
12 Which theoretical approach is supported by the differences in the US and UK constitutions and their impact on civil rights campaigns?

Answers on p. 128

Summary

You should now have an understanding of:
- the similarities and differences regarding the protection of rights in the USA and the UK, particularly the impact of the different constitutions, the role of the judiciary and the importance of the rule of law
- the nature of debates about civil rights in both countries, including the reasons why race, gun rights and religion play a more important role in US politics
- the methods, influence and effectiveness of civil rights campaigns in the USA and the UK, including use of judicial review, lobbying and political campaigning
- the theoretical approaches – structural, rational and cultural – and how each can be used to analyse civil rights campaigns in the USA and the UK.

Exam practice

1 Explain and analyse three ways in which structural theory could be used to study the protection of rights in the USA and the UK.   [9]
2 'The UK Supreme Court has far less power to protect citizens' rights than the US Supreme Court.' Analyse and evaluate this statement.   [25]
3 'Civil rights campaigns have been more effective in the USA than in the UK.' Analyse and evaluate this statement.   [25]

Answers and quick quizz online

ONLINE

Now test yourself answers

Chapter 1

1 Federal.
2 1787, in Philadelphia.
3 Slave states were allowed to count a slave as three-fifths of a free man when calculating the size of their House delegation.
4 Congress, most particularly the Senate.
5 The executive (president).
6 Two-thirds.
7 By making an executive agreement.
8 It allows the Court to strike down laws as being unconstitutional.
9 Robert Bork as a Supreme Court nominee.
10 By co-operating with the president to 'pack' the Court and/or by passing a constitutional amendment
11 (a) Support. (b) Criticism. (c) Criticism. (d) Criticism. (e) Debatable! It depends on one's point of view – there are around 30,000 gun deaths in America, although around two-thirds are suicides. Around 25% of American adults own a gun.

Chapter 2

1 Defense of Marriage Act.
2 US judges are far more powerful and can strike down laws and actions as unconstitutional. UK judges can only declare executive actions *ultra vires* or make a declaration of 'incompatibility'.
3 UK – it only requires parliamentary legislation.
4 US via mid-term elections, though the UK legislature can more easily check the executive by passing a no-confidence motion; however, this was last successful in 1979.
5 No. While both are bicameral, the second chamber in the UK is unelected, while both are elected in the USA.
6 (a) Structural. (b) Rational. (c) Structural. (d) Cultural. (e) Rational.

Chapter 3

1 435 members of the House of Representatives, 100 senators.
2 Bicameral.

3 The refusal by the president to sign a bill passed by Congress. This means the bill does not become law.
4 The charging of a public official with a crime. The charge is brought by the House of Representatives and the Senate is responsible for carrying out the trial and finding the official guilty/not guilty.
5 A tactic whereby a senator (or senators) talk at length to prevent the Senate from voting on a bill, so it cannot become law. Senators have a right to uninterrupted debate, which allows them to use this method of delaying legislation.
6 Cloture is the procedure for ending a filibuster. Three-fifths of senators need to vote for cloture on legislative bills. A simple majority is needed for federal nominations (including to the Supreme Court).
7 The term for Congress's investigation and scrutiny of the federal government, including the president.
8 Congress's right to raise all revenue (tax). This means that Congress needs to pass all federal budgets and therefore holds the 'purse strings' of the federal government.
9 Senate terms are six years long, compared with two-year terms in the House.
10 Around 20%: 19% of the House and 22% of the Senate.
11 Majority-minority districts are congressional districts in which the boundaries are drawn so that a majority of voters in the district are from the same minority group (e.g. African-Americans). They are important because they make it easier for minority candidates to win seats in the House of Representatives. The House has better representation of minorities than the Senate does.
12 Two – these are both independent senators. Every member of the House of Representatives is either a Republican or a Democrat, as are all the other senators.
13 Majority leaders lead the majority parties in each chamber; minority leaders lead the minority parties in each chamber. They are elected by the party caucuses for each chamber.
14 This is the most high-profile leadership position in Congress. The Speaker presides over debates and keeps order in the House, decides on the

legislative agenda for the House, and chooses members of conference and select committees.

15 Permanent committees with a specific policy focus. They can perform the committee stage of bills if the legislation in question involves their policy area. They are also used for oversight and investigation of the government. In practice, much of their work is done in sub-committees.

16 The House Rules Committee sets the 'rules' for bills, determining how much time they will be given on the floor of the House and whether amendments will be allowed. This gives it enormous influence over which bills are likely to be passed and control over the extent to which draft legislation may be altered by Congress.

17 The power to confirm executive appointments and the power to ratify treaties.

18 Refers to unnecessary spending on expensive projects that will benefit a member of Congress's district or state. This funding is often provided by the government in exchange for the member's support in passing key legislation.

19 Senators have a higher public profile, as (along with another senator) they represent a whole state. There is also a well-trodden path from the Senate to the presidency.

20 Congress can pass a constitutional amendment to overturn any Supreme Court ruling. However, this is very difficult to do as two-thirds of both houses need to vote for the amendment and it then needs to be ratified by three-quarters of the states.

Chapter 4

1 Inherent powers.
2 Executive order.
3 Commander-in-chief of the military and the right to negotiate treaties.
4 The Senate.
5 Since 1941, presidents have simply engaged in military action without asking Congress to declare war.
6 A conservative-majority Supreme Court is more likely to make judgements that support a Republican president and a liberal-majority Court is more likely to find in favour of a Democrat president.
7 Cabinet.
8 The chief of staff.
9 The National Security Council (NSC).
10 Richard Nixon's.
11 The Democrats lost control of the House of Representatives: Obama faced divided government for the rest of his tenure.

12 His daughter and son-in-law were both given key positions as his advisers.

Chapter 5

1 Prime minister.
2 President.
3 Prime minister.
4 President.
5 Prime Minister's Question Time.
6 Parliament – via a vote of no confidence in the House of Commons.
7 Prime minister.
8 Prime minister.
9 President.
10 Structural theory.
11 Tony Blair.
12 The size of the parliamentary majority, or lack of one.

Chapter 6

1 Nine.
2 The Senate Judiciary Committee.
3 The Senate.
4 The Senate had a majority of Republicans, who did not want Obama to appoint a liberal justice. They refused even to consider Garland's nomination. The seat remained vacant until President Trump's nominee, Neil Gorsuch, was appointed in 2017.
5 Strict constructionists or originalists.
6 Loose constructionists.
7 The Eighth Amendment, in relation to the death penalty.
8 The First Amendment, freedom of speech.
9 Judicial review.
10 Judicial activism.
11 Judicial restraint.
12 Anthony Kennedy.
13 'Separate but equal'.
14 Same-sex marriage.
15 *Roe* v *Wade* (1973).
16 *Planned Parenthood* v *Casey* (1992) allowed some regulation of abortion; *Gonzales* v *Carhart* (2007) ruled that the Partial-Birth Abortion Ban Act (2003) was constitutional. Both judgements were effectively limiting abortion rights. However, in *Whole Woman's Health* v *Hellerstedt* (2016), the Court ruled against excessive restrictions on abortions, indicating its continuing support for *Roe* v *Wade*.

Chapter 7

1 US justices.
2 US justices.
3 US Supreme Court.
4 US Supreme Court.
5 *Ultra vires*.
6 Twitter criticism by President Trump in 2017 and 2018.
7 The *Daily Mail*'s 'Enemies of the People' headline.
8 The structural approach.
9 The cultural approach.

Chapter 8

1 Ford, Carter and George Bush Senior.
2 War on terror/security.
3 Republicans.
4 Adverts on social media.
5 Hillary Clinton.
6 Ballot initiatives/propositions.
7 Legalising marijuana, same-sex marriage and state minimum wages. Other initiatives have included state taxes, local gun laws and even the wearing of condoms in porn films.
8 No, it's on the decrease.
9 California.
10 State legislatures, though voters can petition for a popular referendum.
11 (a) Democrat. (b) Republican. (c) On balance, probably Republican. Many socially conservative Hispanics may well vote Republican. (d) Democrat. (e) Debatable. Although the majority of LGBT Americans vote Democrat, there are of course exceptions and everything else in this profile suggests a typical Republican voter. Beware of pigeon-holing voters too easily!

Chapter 9

1 Republican.
2 Democrat.
3 Democrat.
4 Republican.
5 Democrat – this is not mentioned in Table 9.2, but be aware that some Republicans are not entirely convinced about the reality of climate change and global warming. Democrats, by contrast, are most likely to oppose measures such as offshore drilling and to promote a reduction in reliance on traditional fossil fuels.

6 (a) False: the number of Blue Dogs has fallen in recent elections. (b) False: there are the Hill committees and the DNC and RNC. (c) True. (d) True. (e) False: that honour belonged to President Trump in 2018.

Chapter 10

1 (a) Republicans and Conservatives. (b) Democrats and Labour. (c) Republicans. (d) Arguably, all the parties except the Republicans. (e) Conservatives and Labour. Only a small proportion even of Democrats would support a mainly state-run healthcare system. (f) Democrats and Labour. (g) Arguably, all four parties, though Labour has always had a strong unilateralist wing, e.g. Jeremy Corbyn. (h) Republicans. (i) Republicans, especially under Trump, and arguably with regard to the EU, pro-Brexit Tories. (j) Republicans and Conservatives. Both parties might be considered more nationalist than their main rivals.

Chapter 11

1 (a) Sectional/interest. (b) Sectional/interest. (c) Cause/promotional. (d) Cause/promotional. (e) Cause/promotional.
2 Pressure group, federal/state bureaucracy and elected legislators.
3 Co-ordinate its campaign with that of the candidate.
4 Speechnow and Citizens United.
5 The civil rights movement.
6 First Amendment rights.

Chapter 12

1 The UK, at least until Brexit.
2 By submitting an *amicus curiae* brief to the court.
3 The UK, but generally only under Labour governments.
4 Hard to say, probably best to say both countries are equal, though corporate interests are certainly more highly organised in the USA.
5 The USA – First Amendment rights and court decisions such as Citizens United.

Chapter 13

1 The Constitution.
2 The First Amendment.
3 Equal protection.
4 *Roe* v *Wade* (1973).

5 *Obergefell* v *Hodges* (2015).

6 The National Rifle Association (NRA).

7 Pro-choice.

8 *Amicus curiae* brief.

9 The American Civil Liberties Union (ACLU).

10 The Equal Rights Amendment (ERA).

11 *Brown* v *Board of Education of Topeka* (1954).

12 The civil rights movement.

13 Affirmative action.

14 Five times greater.

15 The police.

Chapter 14

1 US Supreme Court.

2 US Supreme Court. Its interpretive judgements can be overridden only by a formal amendment to the Constitution, or by a subsequent Supreme Court decision.

3 Human Rights Act (1998).

4 USA PATRIOT Act (2001).

5 The Prevention of Terrorism Act (2005 – repealed 2011).

6 Abortion.

7 The UK (Same Sex Couples) Act (2013) – in the USA it was legalised by the Supreme Court decision in *Obergefell* v *Hodges* (2015).

8 The USA.

9 The USA.

10 That civil rights legislation infringes on their right to oppose certain practices or behaviours because of their religion, e.g. homosexuality.

11 The rule of law.

12 Structural theory.